Bristol 1809
A Fatal Duel

The fugitive's story

editors
Tim Rooth and
Alexander Hallawell

First published in 2013 by Redcliffe Press Ltd.,
81g Pembroke Road, Bristol BS8 3EA
www.redcliffepress.co.uk
info@redcliffepress.co.uk

© Tim Rooth and Alexander Hallawell

ISBN 978-1-908326-26-3
British Library Cataloguing-in-Publication Data
A catalogue record for this book is available from the British Library

All rights reserved. Except for the purpose of review, no part of this book may be reproduced, stored in a retrieval system, or transmitted, in any form or by any means, electronic, mechanical, photocopying, recording or otherwise, without the prior permission of the publishers.

Cover design by Jack Willingham and Stephen Morris
Layout and typesetting by Stephen Morris www.stephen-morris.co.uk
Adobe Garamond 11.8/11.8
Printed and bound by Short Run Press Ltd, Exeter

Contents

Acknowledgements 5

Introduction 7

Chapter 1   A duel: death and the flight of Henry Smith 11

Chapter 2   The shuttlecock of fate 24

Chapter 3   Portugal 48

Chapter 4   Lisbon and the Road to Elvas 62

Chapter 5   Spain, Wellington and the British Army 77

Chapter 6   The Black Watch, Ann and Return to Bristol 96

Postscript   Gordon House, Brighton, 1st March 1909 108

Chapter 7   Henry Smith: his family, friends and profession 113

Appendix 1   The nun's escape 128

Appendix 2   A note on duelling in Great Britain 131

Appendix 3   Dramatis Personae 134

Notes   138

Bibliography 143

Acknowledgements

In preparing this volume we have had help from many people and would like to take this opportunity to thank them.

We are greatly indebted to the Kenneth Spencer Research Library of the University of Kansas for providing access to Henry Smith's diary and particularly to Dr Karen Cook for all her help to Tim Rooth on his visit to Kansas to inspect it. We would also like to thank Miriam Wallen, whose painstakingly prepared typescript of the diary has proved invaluable.

Another key document has been the defence brief held in the archives of Burges Salmon and we are grateful to the firm for letting us see the original document, the oldest in their archives, and to Martin Davies, former senior partner of Burges Salmon, who arranged for a typescript to be made of it.

The Province of Bristol Freemasons gave us access to their records where the late Robert Whalley was particularly helpful in locating the relevant papers. The Province has also given permission to reproduce the portraits of Henry Smith and of Ann as well as the Wanted Poster which was discovered and purchased by Charles Wallis-Newport, a great find.

Dr Rory Muir of the University of Adelaide kindly read an earlier draft and gave useful advice and some welcome encouragement.

We have also benefited from the valuable suggestions of Dr Graeme Davis, Research Fellow at the University of Buckingham.

Paul Rooth, Henry's last surviving great-grandchild until his death in December 2012, was also very helpful in providing copies of family papers, memoirs and other documents which have assisted in the preparation of this volume.

We would like to thank our cousin Anne Hicks of Bristol for all her enthusiasm, help and encouragement over the years. She shared with us many stories that had been passed down to her through the generations concerning Henry and Ann and was able to provide us with pictures, documents and other important clues that allowed us to piece the story together. Without her assistance, indeed, this book would not have been possible. Our thanks also go to her family for their help and unfailing hospitality on our many visits to Bristol. We would also like to acknowledge the very valuable help provided by Anne's grandson Jack Willingham in photographing the poster and three of the portraits which have been included in this volume.

We have encountered much friendliness and help in libraries and archives, notably in the Bristol Central Library, the Bristol Record Office and from the staff of the University of Bristol Library's Kathleen Barker Collection.

It has been a pleasure to work with John Sansom and Clara Hudson of Redcliffe Press and with Stephen Morris.

Alexander thanks his wife, Olcay, and his family for all their help and support during the preparation of this book. Iris Rooth has in a sense had to live with Henry Smith and has given enormous help in numerous ways. Her professional expertise was invaluable in reading earlier manuscripts and making many valuable suggestions about the presentation of the material She has also accompanied Tim Rooth across Portugal and into Spain in tracing the footsteps of Henry Smith (and his grandson), journeys which have often taken them off the more frequented routes.

Introduction

In 1809 Henry Smith was a 34-year-old attorney with a commission in the Bristol Royal Volunteers. He was a member of a family with strong Bristol connections. His father, a very colourful character, had been senior surgeon at the Bristol Royal Infirmary, a position Henry's brother, Richard, later also held. His mother was a member of the well-known Catcott family.

On 1 March, 1809 his life changed forever.

At dawn Henry and Richard Priest, accompanied by their seconds, fought a duel near the Montague Hotel, Kingsdown. We have only Henry's side of the story of the events leading to the duel and the duel itself. Priest was a businessman, described in the Bristol directories as a woollen draper, mercer and undertaker of 9, Clare Street, Bristol. He appears to have been a respected member of the community and in 1807 had been chosen warden of the Antient Guild [later, Society] of St. Stephen's Ringers. Like Henry he was also a member of the Bristol Royal Volunteers, although there is no indication that the two men had known each other before their fateful encounter two days earlier at the theatre.

At the signal shots were fired, Priest was hit in the thigh and, later that morning, died from loss of blood. Henry was unhurt but that afternoon, following a coroner's inquiry, he was indicted for wilful murder. Urged by friends he was persuaded to flee Bristol. With the police in close pursuit he set off for London. Within days posters appeared offering a reward of 100 guineas for his arrest.

This book is an account of this flight. He was on the run for a year, finally returning to Bristol in April 1810 to stand trial. During this time he kept a diary of his travels and misadventures which took him to London, back to Bristol, to Scotland and the Iberian Peninsula where he joined Wellington's army. Before he was able to see action with the Black Watch, however, he was joined by the 19-year-old Ann Creedy whom he had known in Bristol and who had followed him alone to Portugal. Persuaded by her to return, they travelled to Lisbon and then set off for England, returning early in 1810. The diary ends with the trial.

Henry's story has had some publicity in Bristol over the years, partly based on very thin contemporary newspaper reports and later supplemented when his defence brief surfaced from the archives of solicitors Burges Salmon in 1909.[1] However, what has been missing until recently has been the diary. There were rumours of its existence, and it has now been located at the University of Kansas.[2] The account that follows is based largely on the diary.

Disappearance and rediscovery of the diary

Henry's original diary was probably written up later from notes made at the time. It seems likely that the original journal was left to Henry's younger daughter Elizabeth and that this was what prompted his elder daughter Augusta to copy the entire document (including illustrations) in 1863-7, dedicating it to her infant son, Henry Goodwin Rooth (1861-1928). Of the original, Elizabeth treasured it until her death in 1917, when it was inherited by her eldest son John.[3] It has probably not survived but if it has its current whereabouts are unknown.

The copy made in the 1860s was passed down to Henry Goodwin Rooth and his descendants. It was this copy that Rooth used as the basis for his centenary trip to Portugal and Spain in his grandfather's footsteps in 1909, when he and his wife Beatrice travelled across a Portugal still in many ways as poor and remote as it had been a century before: a land where the motor car was barely known outside Lisbon and foreign travellers virtually unheard of beyond the main cities. He also kept a journal of his own and took the opportunity to paint and photograph many of the sights his grandfather and namesake had seen, most of them more or less unchanged.[4]

The story of Henry and his duel became part of the family legend and was passed down the generations, becoming somewhat embellished with time (such as the story that he had fought at Waterloo) but, before it could be properly studied and transcribed, the diary vanished. The only explanation for this disappearance that was ever proffered was that it 'must have been lost in a house move'. Years of searching by various family members among a number of museums and collections proved fruitless and it seemed as if the diary, and with it the details of Henry's remarkable story, had been lost forever. Even with the advent of the internet, the ubiquity of the surname 'Smith' proved a great hindrance to any progress.

Finally, however, in the autumn of 2005, a breakthrough was made and the diary was discovered safe and sound in the collections of the University of Kansas. It transpired that the diary had been sold by one of Henry's great-grandchildren to a local bookseller in 1972 and was acquired by the university soon after. Also sold at the same time were a number of original illustrations by Henry Smith. These were not acquired by the university and their whereabouts are sadly now untraceable. An added boon to the discovery of the diary, however, was the fact that it had been transcribed, as part of a research project, by Miriam Wallen: a painstaking and challenging task, given the nature of the handwriting. This transcription has been compared against the original and has been of great assistance in the writing of this book.

Henry Smith as artist

Smith was a capable amateur artist, and some of the paintings and sketches he made while he was in the Peninsula were published as a series of aquatints which are now held in the British Museum and the National Army Museum. The sketches he made of the family property in Fulham while on the run in March 1809 were donated by his grandson John Rooth to Fulham Library and are still preserved in the borough archives. Bristol City Museum also hold two remarkable illustrations of Henry's on rolls several yards long: *The Coronation Procession of 1821* and an illustration of an election *The Chairing of Henry Bright*, of 1820. Some of his other sketches have survived including one of the house in Queen Square in which he was born and a number of his watercolours have been preserved by the family.

Sources

The major source is the diary. This gives a full and quite detailed account of Henry's travels and misadventures up until just after Ann's arrival in Elvas. Thereafter it is disappointingly terse. We have paraphrased it but kept closely to the original manuscript (modern spelling and punctuation have been used). Some detail, especially of descriptions of scenery, has been edited out. The other important source, used heavily for chapters one and six, has been the defence brief. This was prepared by Daniel Burges, Henry's friend and solicitor, and the original, in a fine copperplate hand, is in the archives of the firm of Burges Salmon. Martin Davies, former senior partner of the firm, arranged for a typescript to be made of this, Burges Salmon's oldest surviving document.[5] We have also used the papers of Henry's brother, Richard Smith, which are in the Bristol Record Office: these were particularly helpful in writing chapter seven.[6] Contemporary newspaper reports have been used but coverage of the trial was rather brief probably because it was overshadowed by the salacious details emerging from the trial the previous day of Sir Henry Lippincott on charges of rape.

Chapter One

A duel: death and the flight of Henry Smith

Dawn, 1 March 1809, Kingsdown

We inspected the pistols. Richard Priest's were too small, so we agreed to use the ones that Peter Clissold had brought on my behalf. Peter loaded them and after Priest and his second had made their choice of weapon we paced out our ground until we stood fifteen yards apart. At the signal we fired simultaneously. I was unscathed but my opponent fell, my shot having hit him in the thigh. I rushed over, shook his hand and then used my handkerchief to bind the wound. Within a few more moments a carriage arrived at speed carrying Priest's surgeon, Mr Hetling, and his assistant. The surgeon asked for a knife, and after cutting open the boot and small clothes pronounced it was an ugly wound.

We left them there and I returned home to College Street, changed and breakfasted. My good friend Peter broke the news of what had occurred to my mother in as light a language as possible. I then left home and walked to my office in St. Stephen's Avenue little dreaming of the events that were to follow. All seemed well enough – I was alive, unscathed and my opponent appeared to have escaped serious injury. I confined myself to my office where anxious friends soon appeared to inquire of my health and to hear what had happened. In view of what was to transpire I should have kept my counsel. At around midday we heard that Priest had had his leg amputated but was doing well. Within another half-hour or so came the dreadful news that he had expired through the profuse loss of blood which had been permitted.

Fortunately at that moment Peter appeared and our futures became as one. No time was to be lost. In consternation I threw my keys into the care of my friend James Lean, left the office and then walked through bye lanes and clay fields not knowing what course to pursue. The judgement of my friends was more collected. They procured a chaise and by the permission of Henry Hunt,[1] after taking a little refreshment and putting two or three clean articles of apparel in a haversack, we set off for his house in Bath. We arrived there at around three in the afternoon, and, to avoid being traced, quitted the chaise in a side street and walked on to Hunt's house in Walcot Street. He arrived about three hours later with the alarming news that within five minutes of the two of us setting off from Bristol a constable had obtained information of our being in Castle Street, though fortunately reports of the direction of our flight had been contradictory.

We remained in the house until, by around eight, it was dark. To disguise myself I wore a slouched hat and Hunt's large driving coat and I adopted a limp. Then, arm-in arm, Peter and I made our way to the bridge. In the meantime Hunt had been successful in meeting a return chaise for Warminster. Our fears were raised when a group of three or four horsemen came up the road from Bristol at full gallop. We popped into the door of a small ale house as the men drew up just by us. One of them shouted *'This is the wrong road – this is not the proper one, they be gone this way'*, and they set off again, at a gallop, towards Wells.

King Street, 1825, showing Theatre Royal by Thomas Rowbotham
© Bristol's Museums, Galleries & Archives

Two days earlier: Theatre Royal, Bristol, 27 February

We were fugitives from the city of my birth, and our situation was precarious in the extreme. The small incident that had occurred two days previously outside the Theatre Royal should never have been allowed to reach such a tragic conclusion. The Italian opera singer Angelica Catalani is touring the country and last week had appeared for the first time in Bristol. Her visit created great excitement, the reviews had been good, and despite the steep prices, demand for the better seats was high.[2] I had promised to accompany a party of ladies to the second night, on 27th February, but had been delayed in my office. By the time I arrived in King Street a queue of about a hundred had formed stretching back along a passage for fifty yards or so. Seeing my party near the top of the passage I moved slowly towards them, obtaining permission to pass as I went, until I felt a blow on my back. Turning, I confronted a man I had just addressed and whom I discovered to be Richard Priest, a draper and salesman of Clare Street. No doubt looking angry I said *'I do not understand that treatment, Sir, I did not merit it'*. Mr Priest had then replied most intemperately, *'Damn your big looks Sir, who cares for them? I can look as big as you'*. Astonished at such language, momentarily lost for words, but feeling deeply insulted, I looked contemptuously at Priest and told him that he was *'an impertinent puppy'*. I started to move on again but was then loudly, in the hearing of many, accused of being a liar. I went back, intent on striking Priest for making such a dreadful accusation. His wife, however, intervened, exclaiming, *'Pray don't strike my husband'*. *'Madam,'* I replied, *'I am disarmed, but Mr Priest must explain his conduct'*. This he agreed, insisting I should also explain mine, and so we settled on meeting next morning.

On Tuesday morning, accompanied by Peter Clissold, and thinking the dispute could easily be settled, I called on Priest at his house. There Priest told me that I had accused him wrongfully, and that it was his wife who had struck me because I had trodden on her toe. If only I had known that at the time, I said, I would have immediately apologised. I asked him to withdraw the accusation of liar. This he adamantly refused to do, despite repeated requests from my friend and myself. Our entreaties foundering on his recalcitrance, I was eventually driven to having to raise my cane. This I did, holding it a small distance from my opponent and saying *'Thus I clear myself from disgrace'*. We then immediately quitted the house.

Two hours later I was called upon by a Mr Guest, a friend of Priest, and we subsequently arranged that he should meet with Peter. Guest requested an apology from me for the insult offered by raising the cane, and in the absence of such an apology informed Peter that his instructions were to leave a challenge. Since neither could agree who should make the first concession, Guest made the challenge which Peter refused to accept, requesting an adjournment for two hours. Earlier, after some drinks, I had visited the Exchange Coffee Room and said that I had caned a man. *'You'll have a writ against you'* warned one of the members.[3] But it was worse than that. The final meeting that evening, at about eight o'clock, was short. Guest, on Priest's behalf, now demanded separate apologies from me for my conduct at the theatre the previous evening and for raising my cane that morning. Peter remarked that it was only necessary for Guest to say that if Priest would withdraw the word 'liar' I would apologise for everything. This was peremptorily refused, and Guest then gave a verbal challenge requiring both parties to meet at seven the next morning, Wednesday.

The duel and the death of Richard Priest

This morning I was still so hopeful that we could avoid a duel that I did not arrange to take a medical man, despite passing the house of my brother Richard, an eminent surgeon, en-route to the appointed place by the Montague Hotel. Indeed, Guest protested to Peter that I should give way because Priest had a wife and child while I had neither.[4] Further attempts at resolving the dispute by mutual apology foundered on my insistence that the slur of liar must be withdrawn before I apologised and Priest's refusal to do so. At this point pistols were produced by each party; although both of us were members of the militia, neither had fired such weapons before.

We both fired and Priest fell. My first emotion was a surge of relief that I had escaped unscathed. Nor, thankfully, did it appear that my opponent was very badly hurt. My time as my father's apprentice had given me some knowledge of medicine and surgery, and I thought it was advisable to bind the wound. But although the surgeon, when he appeared, pronounced the wound ugly, there was no blood and surprisingly they chose not to apply a tourniquet. We then left the ground and

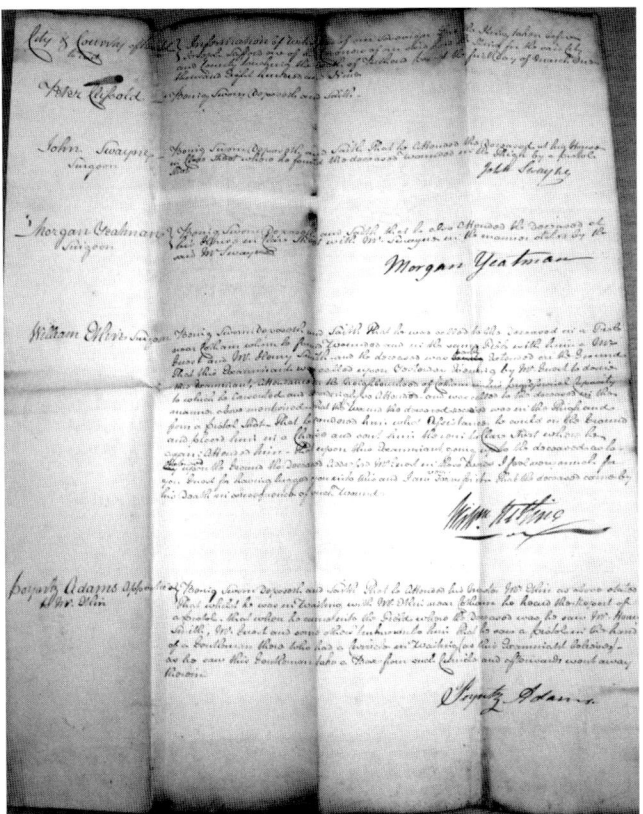

The surgeons' evidence. Bristol Record Office

returned to the city. Apparently, after we departed, Hetling had gone to inform Mrs Priest of what had happened and to summon further medical help. Meanwhile his assistant Adams accompanied Priest, who was very thirsty and occasionally losing consciousness, back to his house. They arrived just before 10, and were shortly joined by two other surgeons.[5] We heard that the leg was badly swollen by then and a tourniquet now put on for the first time. It was decided that the only chance of Priest surviving was to amputate his leg. He died, as I recorded earlier, shortly afterwards.

An inquest was held later in the day, just hours after Priest's unfortunate demise. Before his death Priest had refused to reveal the name of his opponent, none of the witnesses could prove who had inflicted the wound, and the seconds, of course, had wisely disappeared. I'm told that just as the jury was about to return a verdict of wilful murder against some person or persons unknown, my friend William Cornish (whose tea business is in the same street as Priest's and to whom I had recounted events) appeared and, under the impression he was helping me, repeated what he had been told. The jury no longer hesitated but returned a verdict of 'wilful murder against the Defendant and the two seconds and other persons unknown'.

A wanted man

Thus I become a wanted man, as did my second, Peter Clissold, both of us likely to face charges of murder. Hence our nervousness as we left Henry Hunt's house in Bath, a nervousness only heightened by the galloping horsemen who were clearly seeking to apprehend us. After this narrow escape we continued to the bridge. I had decided to go first to Warminster where I had relatives. The chaise soon appeared and, with pounding hearts, we climbed into it. Hunt gave me a letter, addressed to a friend of his, Mr Robert Bird, an attorney in Andover.

It was a bitterly cold night as we set off for Warminster and I was glad of the borrowed greatcoat. We arrived about two in the morning and found a room but sleep eluded us. It was less than twenty-four hours since the duel, Richard Priest was dead and here I was, wrenched from a comfortable life in Bristol and now facing an uncertain future as a fugitive. At around 4 a.m. there was a violent clanging of the gate bell and the trampling of horses' hooves. I gently raised the window to catch any sound, but my alarm proved groundless. We rose at seven and went to my relative, John Bleeck, only to find him still in bed. But we were given a hospitable reception, and then spent the rest of the morning committing to paper every detail of what had happened: in case of separation our stories had to tally. Following dinner and, to raise our spirits, a welcome glass of good wine, we left in a chaise for Andover. We arrived there about eight in the evening, found beds and then, exhausted and feeling more secure now we were further from Bristol, slept well.

Robert Bird, Hunt's friend, proved sympathetic and helpful. To cover our tracks he advised us to travel on to Winchester, spend the night there and then double back to Whitchurch. He had a friend who lived nearby and in the meantime he would prepare the way. Largely to avoid travelling by daylight we stayed on in Andover for dinner where we were joined by Hunt, who fully approved the plan.

We spent the Friday night in Winchester and had time the next morning to explore the cathedral. I decided that I needed to bolster my disguise, and so had a green shade made to cover one of my eyes. I clearly convinced the milliner I needed an eye-patch for she also gave me a recipe, adding that an old aunt who resided at Plymouth had cured a number of our poor fellows who had returned from Egypt with ophthalmia. We then ordered a chaise for Whitchurch, arriving there early in the afternoon. It is a poor small country town with nothing much to recommend it.

I had heard it told that Henry Hunt was by no means universally popular in the district, but clearly he had some good friends and was able to provide Peter and myself with the seclusion we needed. We first stayed for a few days at Upper Henly with John Andrew, a farmer and formerly a major in the militia. He had a small brick house looking onto a farmyard surrounded by old barns, and it was as retired as the desert of Arabia. Our host was a large man, tall with a good corporation and a face that bespoke rude health. If we had not been weighed down by anxieties about our future the stay would have been very pleasant. Our hosts did everything to make us welcome. The major spent the mornings shooting and examining his farm, and in the evenings we listened to music (the eldest daughter played the harpsichord) or formed a hand at cards.

In this pleasant retirement two good Bristol friends, James Lean the banker and Dan Burges, a fellow attorney, contrived to track us down. I had to decide what course of action to take. Should I continue in hiding or go back to Bristol? My first thoughts were that it was best to return and to face trial, and so it was the arrangements for this that we had to put in place. On Thursday 9th March, with heavy hearts, we quitted the place where so much kindness and hospitality had been shown us, and moved on to Sans Souci, a cottage Hunt had had built on his land for sporting purposes. We stayed there for the next three nights. Our time was spent principally in fishing – there was a beautiful wide trout stream – but I devoted the Saturday morning to making a sketch of the cottage and surrounding scenery.

If I was to stand trial I first needed to consult lawyers in London. So, on Sunday 12th, having received a supply of fresh clothes, we set off: we walked to Whitchurch, then took a chaise to Andover and from there boarded the evening coach to London. It was seven in the morning by the time we reached Holborn. Having refreshed ourselves at the Bolt and Tun[6] we visited my agent, Thomas Heelis, whose chambers were nearby

The Staple Inn courtyard. Courtesy Institute of and Faculty of Actuaries (IFOA)

at the Staple Inn. Safety was paramount, and my agent's chambers were a likely spot for the police to search for me. Heelis thought we should be perfectly safe in Chelsea, so we set off in a hack and after a long search managed to find lodgings in Eaton Place. There we were soon visited by my old master, Robert Payne, now living in London, and frequent visits by Payne and Heelis served to distract us from the dire situation we were in. It was now nearly a month since the duel. On the 27th my brother Richard arrived from Bristol, accompanied by Burges. Next day Richard and I visited Fulham where the family had property. It was a filthy day, and we got soaked to the skin, but I did find time to make some sketches and plans of the house.[7]

Return to Bristol: a midnight ruffian

On Monday 3rd April we held legal consultations at Counsellor John Gurney's Chambers dealing mainly with the arrangements for my surrender. It was agreed that I would travel back to Bath and meet friends there on Saturday. On Wednesday, having told people at the lodgings that I was going to Norfolk, I instead set off for Bath, travelling by chaise to Windsor. The next morning I attended service in the King's Chapel

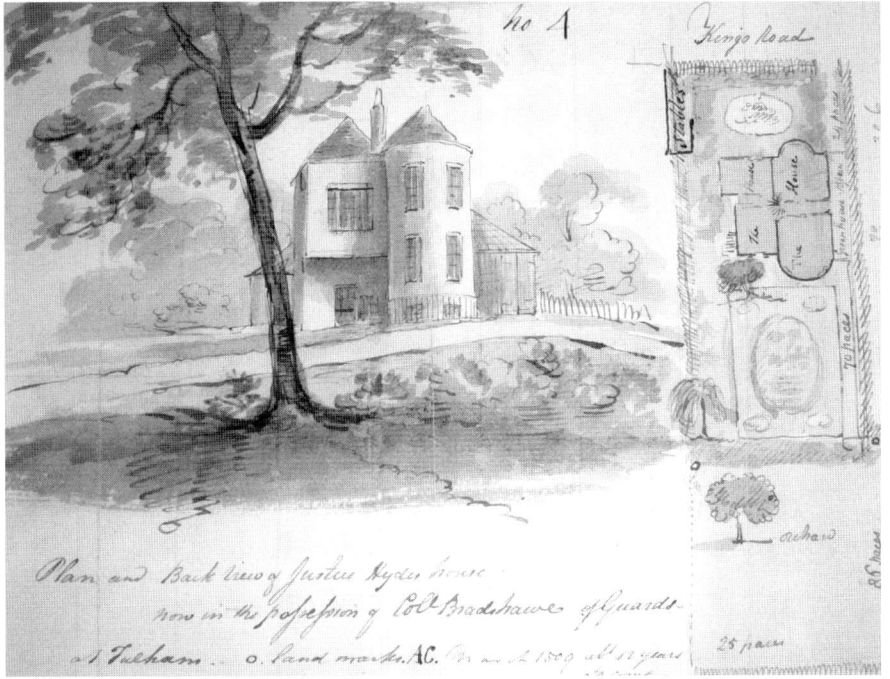

Sketch of the Catcott family properties at Fulham, Middlesex, painted by Henry Smith during his flight, 28th March 1809 ('...a heavy rain wetted us to the skin.').
© Hammersmith and Fulham Archives

and then visited the castle. Here I was the beneficiary of a great act of kindness. Among the visitors to the castle was a young man whose face I knew but was unable to place. As soon as he recognised me he came across, told me with great frankness that he had heard of my misfortunes but assured me that I had nothing to fear from him. We parted, but later in the day, before I had finished dinner, he appeared at my Inn holding a small package, and with every apology, offered a loan of £50, saying my word to my relatives in Bristol would be security enough. This was a large amount of money[8] and, in my distressed state of mind I was so overcome by such an act of kindness that at first I was unable to speak and could merely shake his hand. I then recognised him: he had been an articled clerk to an attorney, Mr Easton, in Bristol, and told me he was now married and practising in Monmouthshire.

Peter and I travelled on, spending the next night at Hartford Bridge and the following one at Andover. It was here that we had agreed to separate. The next morning, the 8th April, I left him still in bed, and set off

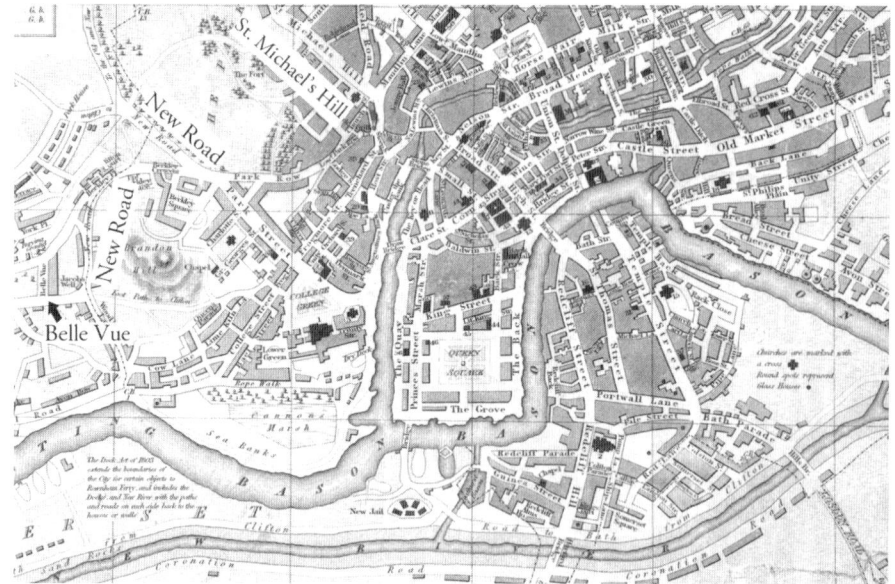

Detail from Bristol map 1828 © Bristol's Museums, Galleries & Archives

to Bath by stage coach. I arrived there at about eight in the evening and an hour later was joined by Lean and Burges; the three of us then travelled by chaise to Bristol. As we approached the city Lean and Burges emphasised the dangers that I faced in returning to Bristol and the representations of my friends made my mind alive to every fear. According to the plan I left the chaise in Totterdown and, wrapped in Lean's greatcoat, made my way on foot to his house in Belle Vue. The night was peculiarly dark. I armed myself with a good stick and resolved that if I was to be arrested it would need more than one person to apprehend me. I set off towards Temple Gate, but, hearing two people talking together, I changed my mind and, instead, returned to the canal. I stumbled over stones and heaps of rubble before at last arriving in Bedminster Road. It felt strange and disturbing to be returning to my native city as a fugitive, and it was dreadful to have to steal through it like a midnight ruffian, fearing at every corner I might encounter an officer.

Since I would have been familiar to most of the City Watch I attempted to disguise myself by walking lame. I limped up Redcliff Street, crossed the bridge and then climbed the steps by the chapel into Maryport Street and then through the Cornmarket. I crossed Wine Street into Tower Lane where scarcely a lamp was burning. There, as I was cautiously groping my way forward in the dark, I received a violent slap on my shoulder and my right arm was seized. My first instinct was to resist, but turning round I was relieved to find myself alone in the custody of a woman. My fears subsided, but worried that the tone of my voice might be recognised I merely bowed and moved quickly on.

I resolved to avoid St. Augustine's Parish and took an indirect route up St. Michael's Hill, through the park [Tyndall's Park] and into New Road [today's Queen's Road]. A door in New Road [at this point Jacobs Wells Road] opened into the gardens of Belle Vue. My instructions had been clear. Lean had given me the key to the gardens, and I was to come cautiously through them, get into Lean's adjoining private garden and to wait there until called. Having opened the door into the first garden, I was stealing through the shrubberies to my hiding place when I saw something dark like a human figure move from behind a large bush. I froze, gripped my stick firmly and watched intently. Nothing moved. At last, feeling the uncertainty was worse than whatever might happen, I took a huge sideways step and again stood still. The figure moved too. Convinced there was somebody near me I had resolved to fight if necessary, only to be greeted by Lean. Holding my friend's arm I crept into my hiding place while Lean and his servant (whose fidelity and attachment I knew I could depend upon) reconnoitred. All was clear and I entered the familiar and hospitable house with my heart still pounding.

I spent Sunday there, my cares receding in the company of Lucy, Lean's amiable wife. Indeed it has been my good fortune to excite friendship and sympathy wherever I have sojourned. The household was buzzing with excitement and speculation about my presence, and this had reached the nursery. On the night I arrived an emergency escape route through the garret had been prepared, and this had alerted the maids. Next morning the daughter of the household, scarcely three years old, asked her father *'what about Harry Mif?'* On being questioned she said she had overheard Jane the nursemaid speak my name and she wanted to know where Harry Mif was.

A change of plan: defying the court
The assizes were to open next morning, so that evening was to decide my immediate fate. Vital decisions had still to be taken, and at eight a consultation was held in the house, attended by my defence counsellors

Pill and Joseph Smith. All present attempted to persuade me to postpone the dreadful day but I was determined to appear. I had made my mind up to face the court and I was prepared to meet the law's greatest vengeance. I saw no point in deferring it although argument after argument was used to dissuade me. Yet I felt there was some unspoken factor behind my friends' argument for delay, some cause of which I was unaware. Counsel used an impressive style of language without equally forcible reason. Had there been some intimation from the prosecuting counsel, Mr Lens? He would assist in conducting a just prosecution, but surely not a disgraceful *persecution*? My resolution was unshaken. Only then was the decisive argument deployed: if I persisted it would probably prove fatal to my mother. This was put to me in plain unambiguous language – her health had already been seriously undermined by the events of the past month. That was enough. Pressed by my friends, consumed by guilt and worry about my mother, I conceded.

It was a momentous decision. I would defy the courts and brand myself an outlaw. I was condemning myself to an indeterminate exile from the city, from my family and my friends. I now needed to move quickly. Several strong hints had already been made that it would be imprudent to remain any longer in Belle Vue, and it was decided that I should go to Dan Burges's house in Ashton. At eleven that night I was accompanied by my two friends out through Belle Vue gardens to St. Jacob's Well, and from there I walked with Burges to Rownham Ferry. It took a considerable time to first wake the boatman and then to cross the river which had been choked up by mud from the new canal. We ended up well below the slip and had to clamber up the muddy bank. By the time we reached the cottage it was well after midnight and the family were in their beds. We enjoyed a cigar and a glass of grog before retiring, although with my head still reeling from the events of the day I found sleep elusive.

In the morning Dan Burges went into Bristol on business as usual but when he returned to dinner at five he seemed agitated. During the meal he poured generous glasses of wine and told me to steel myself for making a long journey. I was taken aback but pressed him to tell me the worst.

'Harry, you must set off for London tonight.'

'Is that all?' I said, aghast.

Bristol was in ferment. *'The Guildhall this morning was filled by break of day to hear the trial and you not appearing has excited a fevered sensa-*

1 Belle Vue, Bristol, Home of the Lean family 1809 'There I remained in secrecy…my cares apparently forgotten in the society of his amiable wife.'

tion,' Burges explained. Indeed, he himself had been summonsed into court to answer some questions.

'You will doubtless be looked for here tonight; to stay therefore will be madness. As soon as it is dark you must depart.'

So there it was. I was to be on the move again, two nights after returning to the city. I was thankful that at least my health was good and I had my share of spirit. My friend opened a fresh bottle of good wine, raised a toast to our next meeting, and made sure that my glass was kept topped up.

Chapter 2

The shuttlecock of fate

Bristol to London

As arranged, I left Ashton at about 8 in the evening, just as dusk set in. Parting from Burges's wife and mother was heartbreaking, particularly his mother, Catherine, who had known me from childhood and who shed tears over me like a parent. I was directed to leap the garden wall and make my way over fields to a lane running from the Ashton road to Lady Smyth's at Red Cliff. By now it was very dark, the path narrow and I had to cross a stream bridged by a single plank. When eventually I arrived at the agreed meeting point, I waited for Burges to appear. I was nervous of making any noise, and secreted myself in a dry ditch. In the pitch dark I was hard to locate, and when a horseman passed by I kept quiet. Only when the horseman returned and started muttering to himself that I must have lost my way did I hail my friend. We then made our way through Bedminster before separating at the point where the roads to Dundry and Ashton diverged. Borrowing Burges's horse I was to make my way up the long lane to the Totterdown Turnpike where Lean's servant was to meet me. Again, this was a difficult journey in the dark and involved crossing an unprotected bridge. The lane is about one-and-a-half miles in length, and it was so dark I could barely see the hedge and had simply to trust to the safe foot of the horse. The path truly seemed never-ending. At length, much to my alarm, a horseman passed me and put his face as near mine as possible: 'the thief fears every man an officer', and I construed every person a bailiff. But I was greeted by the familiar voice of Lean's servant who warmly congratulated me on my safety. The voice of sympathy is the best of balms to a heart ill at rest. Dan Burges soon made his appearance and we then set off at a brisk trot for Knowle, and, taking a small lane, came into the Bath road at Brislington.

By the time we arrived it had turned midnight, and we then had a consultation as to the best course to pursue. The Warminster road was the more secure route to London but Warminster itself was 18 miles beyond Bath. It was a dark, dreary night, and I was weary and travelling with a heavy heart. Burges urged the necessity of making the best use of the night. Reluctantly agreeing, I said I was prepared for anything. With that we turned our horses and set off for Warminster. But after galloping 300 yards or so Burges seemed suddenly to sicken at the prospect of the journey. *'You had better have a chaise if it can be procured for the journey.'* I told Burges to go to Banks at the Lamb. Banks was a fellow mason, and I suggested Burges tell him the full story and the extent of my predicament. Meanwhile I concealed myself up a narrow lane. Apparently Burges had barely begun his explanation when Banks interrupted: *'Your fears are for Smith; bring him here, he's safe.'* When I appeared Banks gave me a cordial handshake, and said I had not been out of his mind the whole day. He brought in wine and biscuits and sent for one of his drivers. When the driver appeared Banks pointed to me, asking him if he knew who I was: *'Very well, it's Master Smith.'*

A little before 1 o'clock Banks instructed the driver to saddle the four best horses and *'take him with all speed to Warminster, and provided no horses can be procured there to go on with him another stage.'* The driver, as he turned, said *'I'll be damned if anybody comes near him whilst in my chaise.'* The driver cracked on at great pace. I had no greatcoat and lay crouched up on the seat, my attempts to sleep defeated by the numbing cold and my churning mind. At about four we stopped. I stayed inside until a second chaise appeared and then stepped straight from one vehicle to the other. As we journeyed across Wiltshire I sat shivering inside, a miserable journey made even more uncomfortable by one of the chaise's raves being broken. Daylight brought little relief. The road, running over the uncultivated downs of Wiltshire with barely a tree or shrub in sight, was dreary in the extreme. We arrived in Andover just in time for me to get a roof seat on the long coach to London. When on Wednesday 12th April we finally arrived in the capital I left the coach at the top of Sloane Street in order to avoid being seen and took a hackney to my agent in Chancery Lane. Heelis found me temporary accommodation at Parcival's Inn and the following day accompanied me to Islington where I took a decent lodging for a week.

Wanted for murder

I visited my friends George Donne and his wife in Guildford Street and stayed for dinner but, feeling that I was safer out of town, declined their offer of a bed. Heelis accompanied me back to my new lodging and, attempting to raise my sinking spirits, kept me company until late. When he returned next evening he brought shocking news. Among some papers in a parcel he brought from Bristol was a poster proclaiming that I was wanted for murder! The horror I experienced when reading the document is beyond description: a numbing coldness came over me and I fell senseless to the floor. When at last I revived I read through the advertisement and accompanying letters from Lean and Burges but by this point I had lost all sense and reason. Although I read the letters I made little of their contents and had no idea what to do next. Indeed I imagined that every pillar in London would have my name emblazoned on it.

The net closing in: heading north and the hazards of travel

At least Heelis was there to offer guidance and support and we agreed that next morning I should travel to St. Albans. I spent a sleepless night: the previous evening Heelis's chambers had been closely watched, and with the net closing in it was best not to travel by coach. Next morning Heelis sent his clerk over to help me make my departure, and by 10 o'clock I had set off by chaise on the five-hour journey to St. Albans. Three mail coaches went north every day from here, but I was told that they were generally packed within and without. The first mail, passing through about six, was indeed full, and on the second I only managed to get the last space outside. About 11 it started to pour with rain and the deluge continued without a minute's cessation during the night. Two of my fellow passengers had umbrellas but, without doing much good to the owners these served only to annoy their neighbours. We journeyed through the downpour all that night and all the following day, not arriving in Manchester till 11 the following evening, by which time all the outside passengers were wet through and my clothes, when wrung out, would have yielded some quarts of water. My hat could be folded up and put in my pocket! Taking a warming glass of spirits, I immediately retired to bed, sleeping without interruption till 1 the following afternoon. I awoke, however, with considerable pain and shiverings in my limbs occasioned no doubt by the dampness of my clothes in which I had been sitting so long. Not wishing to linger in Manchester, I left the city as soon as I was able, passing the time by visiting the theatre and leaving on the morning coach for Liverpool in very pleasant society. After some difficulty I eventually discovered lodging at The King's Arms near

Henry Smith's itinerary for England and Scotland, 1809

the Exchange, an excellent house.

I now needed to secure my passage to Canada as quickly as possible and had a letter of introduction for that purpose to a Mr Davies from my friends the Helmars in Bristol. Liverpool being unsafe from the frequent intercourse between that town and Bristol, Mr Davies accompanied me to a village called Wavertree about two miles distant and there procured me a comfortable apartment. The next day, 20th April, Lean and Burges came from Bristol bearing a packet of letters. I retired anxiously to read them. My Bristol associates seemed determined for me to sail to Canada and establish myself in a legal career there. The thought of living thousands of miles from friends and family filled me with horror but it seemed as if I must be resigned to my fate. My friends seem to want me to settle in Canada in the legal department, to which I added my compliance. However, if (as my counsel and all my friends seemed certain) there was to be a trial at the next assizes was it not extremely rash to go so far with no chance of surrendering in time to face the court? It was at this point that a quite different course was suddenly suggested, which was to affect the whole of my future life: joining the Scots or Irish militia. Who first ventured this idea, Lean or myself, I can no longer be sure, but both my friends approved and the die was cast.

Having arranged my departure for Scotland my two friends and I arrived in Liverpool the following evening and at the Liverpool Arms took a long, long farewell. Dan Burges saw me off, seated on the roof of the Carlisle mail. Yet again I had failed to find a seat inside and was forced to endure a purgatorial journey. The night was extremely cold and it was my bearskin coat, I believe, that kept life afloat, for my extremities were literally benumbed. After one night in Carlisle, a hasty dinner was scarce swallowed before the bugle of the guard proclaimed all ready. I could scarcely believe my luck, securing my baggage and placing myself in a snug seat facing backwards. However, this was indeed too good to be true, for suddenly the rough voice of the coacher roared through the window *'which of you gentlemen' he got in here fresh, as here be two that com'd in the London Mail be going on?'* Yet again, poor Pill Garlick[1] was obliged to mount the roof.

Scotland

First impressions of the border country beyond Carlisle were not encouraging. The country is still dreary and inhospitable, principally consisting of black peat-heath. Even at this moment, though, it was hard not to be intrigued by the ruins of the ancient peel towers which litter the landscape. At about 5pm we crossed the tiny rivulet that separated England from Scotland and entered the celebrated village of Gretna Green. The horn of the guard brought to the door of a low dirty house the person known by the name of the blacksmith, who by the by has lately taken up the trade of tobacconist, which with his other occupation brings pretty good grist to the mill. As it grew dark absolute exhaustion took hold of me and several times I narrowly escaped falling from the roof. It had grown bitterly cold. Twelve hours later we were still travelling as a heavy Scotch mist descended, but the romance of the scenery still beguiled me, vast glens through which we distinctly heard the torrents from the mountains dashing, forming at intervals deep and wide lakes. Dark forests of fir clothed the mountainside. We passed close to the seat of the Duke of Hamilton, set among thick forest. Finally, at 7 on Tuesday morning, the coach with its weary passengers wound its way into Glasgow.

On my long journey, I had made the acquaintance of a Mr Carasaw, of 12, Fish Street Hill, London and this fellow suffering traveller took me to the Tontine Inn, then considered the best in the town, situated in the principal street over the public coffee house.[2] The inn is certainly very large but dirt and filth is more protected there than I ever remember to have seen. Despite containing accommodation for over two hundred people, with spacious dining- and bed-rooms, yet the small space of three or four feet could not be found to erect a most essential convenience particular to an Englishman. The waiters to be sure boast of an excellent one, but conceive how expectation is fulfilled when he shows you a recess near the stable, in the common yard and open to every stable boy that chooses to use it. Females must find it a most inconvenient house. Wandering around town later I noticed the high tenements, 6 or 7 storeys in places, and how onc has to stretch the neck to the utmost to see a tradesman's sign hanging from the top floor. Some parts of the city were remarkably similar to Bath in their architecture, but my attention was drawn particularly to the High Kirk, built in the 'Forest Gothic' style of the High Middle Ages but where the solemn chant of the monks no longer resounds. There were fine stone bridges crossing the wide Clyde River and desirable residences lately built on the opposite bank.

After a disappointing night at the theatre, on Thursday morning (29th), now refreshed in spirits, I mounted the mail for Greenock, 21 miles away. Passing the ruins of Cranston Castle one could not help ruminating on the tragic story of Mary Queen of Scots and Darnley, the site of whose first tryst was marked by the withered stump of an old fir tree. There every traveller carries away a slip of the tree with as much belief in the fable as the Catholic puts faith in the bit of wood handed down from generation to generation as a precious relic of the cross (which if they could be collected would be sufficient to build a first-rate man of war). Passing the ancient rock of Dumbarton I saw towering above its neighbours Old Ben Lomond. In front, the Clyde widening as it approaches the sea, on the left the town of Port Glasgow and Greenock and in the distance the blue hills of Argyle, the whole enlivened by the numerous vessels passing in every direction.

The legs of our northern neighbours

Arriving in Greenock, a small but very neat place, I was delighted with my new accommodation at another Tontine Inn.[3] It has every comfort that is to be met with in our best English houses, extremely clean and the beds are of the first order. There is no coffee room but a kind of public room for travellers where I took up my abode. Being alone, I spent the first two or three days strolling round the town. I saw very many pretty faces among the females but I was perturbed to discover that the ladies wear nothing but stockings and shoes on their legs, which to a stranger have a very filthy appearance; the legs of our northern neighbours are not their best feature. Not being able to find a house which took in lodgers, I was obliged to stay at the inn for nearly a week, which was proving a burdensome expense. I spent my days walking in the surrounding hills, quite alone except for the occasional solitary shepherd whose dog seemed astonished at my presence. I did not intend to stay long in Greenock and was expecting daily some intelligence from home that might command me to change my residence, so I determined to see Loch Lomond before I went. On the first of May early in the morning I took boat; the sea was very rough and a stiff gale of wind blew. A boat cloak, which one of the men lent me, kept me dry, though they both had a complete washing. Touched by their kindness, I tried to reward them with two good glasses of whisky and took a small one myself before starting the next stage of the journey. The scene as the loch opened up before me was enchanting, on every side sublime vistas strike the eye and ravish the heart of the admiring visitor. Ben Lomond consists entirely of rock and scanty herbage which affords food for the numerous goats that the traveller sees skipping from rock to rock where a single false step must head it to perdition. Beyond this mountain rises a range of others whose summits are peaked in most fantastic forms and, though the day was remarkably warm, yet their tops were clothed with snow.

Sketching

I seated myself on the bank of the lake, under the shade of a pine tree and almost for the first time divested myself of the remembrance of my misfortunes. I was suddenly struck by a sense of loneliness, and I only wished for one sympathising being who would participate in my happiness. Having made a few sketches, hunger overtook me and I returned to the Luss Inn to enjoy their excellent bacon and eggs. Feeling perhaps that I had lingered too long and wishing to hear news from my friends, I decided to make a 'forced march' to Dumbarton, where I arrived about 9 o'clock that night. I was shown into a miserable back room at the inn and when I remonstrated with the waiter he told me he had just given the last unoccupied room to two young Englishmen who were on a walking tour. I sent in stating my want of a comfortable room and asking whether they had any objection to a brother artist joining them for the evening. They both came to express their pleasure at such an opportunity and we agreed to drink the health of our mutual friends south of the Tweed with a bottle of whisky punch. They were both medical students at Edinburgh and during the vacation had been walking the Highlands – their sketches were but indifferent. In the morning I was delighted to discover that the inn furnished a most excellent breakfast, fish of various kinds pickled and dried, particularly a loch herring which is delicious eating; and eggs in plenty with famous cream, a food that Scotland has long excelled in.

After breakfast we went to the fortress, perched on the Rock of Dumbarton and surmounted by high bastions and several field pieces. Imposing as it is I should look upon it as no very difficult task to scale its flinty walls and it would easily be overcome by a battery situated on a height which was less than half a mile distant. We passed into the fortress through a stout gateway, climbing up to a platform facing the governor's house and overlooking the river. We were shown an immense sword reported to have belonged to William Wallace and two small pieces of brass artillery taken from the Pretender. Behind the governor's house the rock splits in two and a steep flight of sixty or seventy steps ascends in front of you. On either side the rocks hang over to a great height forming almost a Gothic arch. At the top of the flight of steps is a strong narrow doorway, by which a very few soldiers might prevent the passage of twofold their own number. I obtained permission from the governor, as a great favour, to make a sketch, assuring him it was merely for my own use. A hard-favoured highlander, however, stood guard over me all the while.

We crossed the estuary from a little jetty just outside the fortress. We were pulled over against a fresh breeze by the ferryman and his wife, the former a most filthy object; his two legs were covered with disease from the knees to the toes and which I was afterwards informed was the Scotch Fiddle. My companions and I parted on the other side, they going to Glasgow and me to Greenock, where I arrived about 4 o'clock.

The shuttlecock of fate

I wolfed down some dinner and then hurried to the Post Office, desperate for news. No letter! What could be the cause? Had I offended my friends or were they wary of detection? Feeling dreadfully distressed and in a state of complete confusion I wrote at once to a friend in Bristol determined that I would no longer be a plague to my family and friends. A thousand fruitless plans were suggested but none seemed likely to amount to anything. Then in the next post – thank God! – a letter, in the familiar handwriting of my good friend Lean. The plan was, yet again, that I should go to Canada and practise law there, an idea which hardly filled me with joy, but I had long resolved to be the shuttlecock of fate, without a murmur. Feeling that my future course was now fixed I only awaited the orders of my friends to embark, and decided to make the best use of my remaining time, walking to Paisley on the Friday and examining the ruins of the abbey there. In the burial chapel may be heard an astonishing echo, even a whisper being heard distinctly in any part of the building. To show its effects the sexton slams the door, which causes a noise like the report of artillery. Leaving Paisley, I walked the five miles to Crookston, to the somewhat sorry remains of its castle. The setting, however, is certainly beautiful and on every side the surrounding country is picturesque. The poor remnants of a yew tree stand about 150 yards from the castle, and like other travellers I carried away my slip. On the northern side at the base of the hill, over a rocky bottom, flows a beautiful transparent stream – I was induced to make three or four sketches of these noted ruins, which on every side afford food for the artist.

Having spent so long at Crookston, I had no choice but to stay in Paisley the night, where I had a miserable and ill-dressed dinner. I was pleasantly surprised to discover, however, that a Masonic Lodge, the Royal Oak, met nearby and I attended at the door with my brotherly token. I found, however, that very little ceremony was used upon my admittance. Of the mysteries of the 'prison house' I shall follow the first precept of brotherhood: silence. Masonry is at a very low ebb with our Scotch brethren; a lecture is a thing only known by name amongst them. In consequence their meetings often terminate, not as in England 'in the harmony of brotherly love' but in drunkenness and confusion.

New friends

I returned to The Tontine Inn at Greenock, but the expense of the establishment was beginning to take its toll on my purse. On the 8th of May I was fortunate in meeting with a comfortable lodging. My hostess is a Mrs Kerr,[4] a widow woman, who is much respected in the town. I afterwards was informed she had two daughters but they were then absent. A difficulty arose as to my boarding but she told me there was something in my manner that pleased her. In the same house, and which rendered it very pleasant, resided Captain Skelton of the Royal Navy, a gentleman of about forty years of age who had lost the kneepan in the action at Boulogne under Nelson and was consequently unserviceable. He had a room and lived to himself, but it was always open to me. The other lodger was a nephew of our hostess, a good-hearted Lieutenant of the 91st Highlanders, John McDougall. He had never been from his native county, Argyle, and therefore could not know much of the world. We contrived, however, to make time pass merrily on together and here I was informed that my trips to the mountain had obtained me the name of 'the mad Englishman', which used to afford us many a laugh. Our

Old Tontine Hotel, Cathcart Street Greenock where Henry stayed for a week before his departure for the Peninsula ('I had nothing to complain of but the expense'). Built 1801, demolished c.1895 and replaced by the James Watt Inn which now occupies the site. © McClean Museum and Watt Library

hostess was a truly worthy and motherly kind of woman and tried every means to render us happy and comfortable, and to say the truth I do not think the town of Greenock produced three merrier hearts. I had forgotten all my misfortunes and could I have divested my mind of 'Bristol' might have continued there very contented. After I had been there about ten days the young ladies made their appearance. The eldest was pretty; the younger one however seemed the favourite of my fellow lodgers. She was about 18, a fine figure and, in spite of her <u>nose</u>, handsome. A piano which had hitherto been locked up now made the walls echo. Her knowledge, however, only extended to country dances and an old song book.

Meanwhile, my circle of friends continued to grow. My friend Mr Thompson, who seemed to be acquainted with most of Greenock, introduced me to Mr James Lyons,[5] a good-hearted man with whom I began to dine frequently, and Thompson himself did me much honour by taking me to most invitations with him. But he told me that my presence in town had begun to excite a good deal of curiosity, many asking pointedly whether my name was really 'Smith'. Not all were convinced by his assurances, as I soon found to my cost. One morning when the local militia were exercising, an officer by the name of Major Ewing, known as something of a factious 'mad ways', strolled up to me and said *'Well, Captain Smith, what do you think of our men? Don't you think their improvement does their officers credit?'* He proceeded to describe some ridiculous manoeuvre which I cannot now remember, clearly simply to test whether my captaincy was genuine or not. I asked whether he had ever seen, heard or read of such a movement. *'Indeed'*, he replied and marched off, having, I felt, met his match.

A few days later I travelled to Glasgow to see Mrs Jack, the daughter of my good friend from home, Dr Newman. She had married just a few days previously. What a joy to be amongst old friends again: she and her husband made us very welcome in their well-situated new house in Clyde Buildings, on the south side of the city and commanding a charming panorama of the river. We spent five or six days together, reminiscing about Bristol friends, now either absent or departed, and our many happy evenings at The Amphion.[6]

A hurricane of misfortunes and a change of plan: destination Portugal

Imagine my shock when my pleasant time here was cut short when I received word from Mr Thompson that all the arrangements for my departure to Canada had been abandoned (for reasons too long to set forth here) and that my friends believed my best course now was to head to Portugal as soon as may be and join the Patriot Army. This doleful news was followed by what I can only describe as a hurricane of misfortunes. On the 28th I was quietly writing in my room when the guard of the mail appeared, brandishing a letter from Mr Jack. Thank goodness I had decided a few days before to reveal all to Mrs Kerr and Captain Skelton, as suspicions about me were continuing to grow and I felt it was the lesser risk to take them into my confidence. When the guard arrived Skelton had actually drawn his broadsword in my defence, but seeing the letter was quieted and accompanied him to the very door of my room. The letter was from two friends in Bristol, who shall remain nameless at their own request. Some *person* had apparently seen me in Glasgow and sent news to the mayor to have me arrested immediately. I

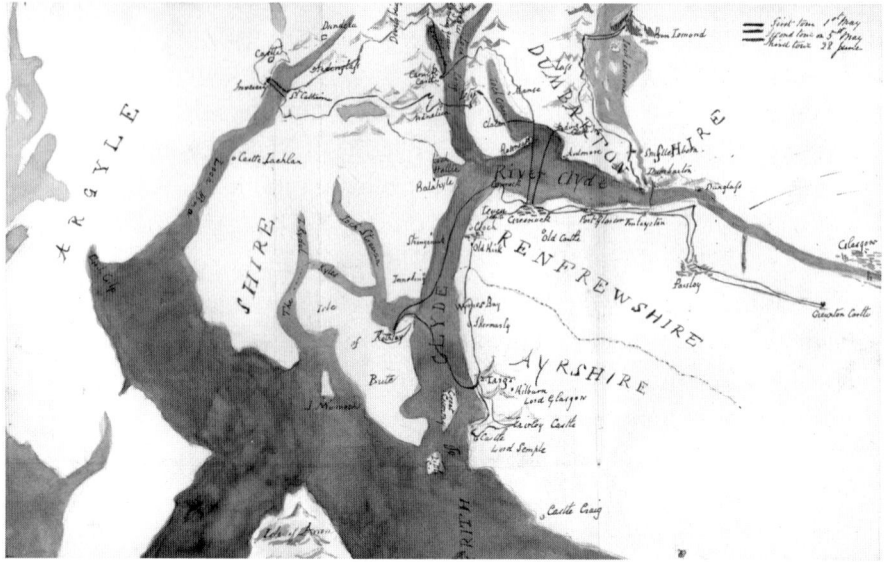

Journeys in Scotland, drawn by Henry Smith. Kenneth Spencer Research Library, University of Kansas

was advised to leave Greenock at once. You can scarcely imagine the scene that ensued: old Mrs Kerr and her daughters and the two servant maids wringing their hands and weeping uncontrollably (the maids with no idea of the reason, of course). It was as if I had been on the road to Tyburn itself. My friend Lyons then arrived with more letters to the same effect and a 'Council of War' was rapidly convened. But what to do? There was no ship to Portugal for three weeks so an interim escape plan was essential: the Isle of Bute. It was foolish, however, to take ship from Greenock so we made haste for Wemyss Bay, a little bathing village three miles along the estuary, Skelton and McDougall vowing never to leave me till I was safe and sound. Skelton limping along behind us with his injured knee was hardly conducive to a quick escape so McDougall, my friend Galbraith and I set off at a brisk trot, leaving Skelton in charge of the baggage, carried on the shoulders of a lusty Highlander. Arriving in Gourock about 6, I hastily scribbled two letters in a little ale house: one to Glasgow, one to Bristol, to ease the fears of my friends. Bute lay about eighteen miles distant. The night was very dark and cold, and only an open boat could be secured. Skelton was too much of the old sailor, though, to go to sea upon short allowances and, unknown to me, but to my agreeable surprise, about 9 o'clock produced two bottles of good

Madeira. He had every credit given him for his forethought as the wine completely settled my drooping spirits. Eleven had struck before we set foot on terra firma.

The chief (indeed only) town of Bute, Rothesay, has but one inn, more deserving indeed the title of ale-house, but beggars cannot be choosers and we were glad enough of three beds and some victuals. When, however, the next morning dawned, we were perturbed to discover that not only were the local militia on duty, but that several of the officers were of our acquaintance in Greenock. The major, indeed, insisted we dine with him, much against our inclination, and so our plans for concealment came to nothing. During the day we walked around the town, and I took the chance to paint the ivy-choked ruins of the castle. The next day we thought it prudent to leave Bute as it was not nearly as isolated as we had anticipated.

A filthy immersion

We went to the village of Largs, which has a very good beach and is beautifully situated on a fine bay. But that evening I observed many faces from Greenock so the next morning McDougall and I rose early and, to escape as much observation as possible, agreed to walk and explore the village of Paisley, about three miles down the river. Nearby we came upon Temple Castle, just fifty years since the residence of Lord Temple but now quite ruined, and surrounded by trees. Within two or three cottages had been erected and the inhabitants had placed against the once ornate and noble gateway a certain miserable shed or hut with a straw roof, called a 'necessary': the tall nettles told it had long been without an inhabitant. While I was sketching the gateway, my companion astonished me by exclaiming *'Othello's occupation is gone'.*[7] On looking up I perceived his allusion was to this miserable hut. After a laugh I again returned to my book, paying no attention to what he was about. Scarcely three minutes had elapsed before a tremendous cry from my friend made me spring from my seat: I saw the small ruin tottering and, ere he could make his escape, the roof had fallen in. The seat was so rotten that it gave way and in an instant he became immersed in filth and misery. Fearing he might have received an injury I was considerably alarmed till, on removing the straw roof, which had confined him snug to his seat, I could not for my life have forborne laughing. In the midst of his misfortune he could not help joining in. The noise had brought to their doors many of the cottagers, through whom he had to run the gauntlet till, with the aid of a pump, he began to smell a little sweeter. He swore he would explore no more old buildings and hurried me back to our inn at Fairley, where we had an excellent turbot and beef steak and over a bottle of wine many times laughed at the morning's adventure.

We arrived at Largs at dusk to find a letter from Skelton saying all was well, so the following morning we set out for Greenock through the high lands in order to avoid detection. On my way I was not idle, making two or three drawings of Wemyss Bay and Skelmorlie Castle and stopping for dinner at the village of Old Kirk. When we returned to Mrs Kerr's about 10 that night we were met with the warmest of receptions. The next day I took ship across the Clyde to Ardencaple Inn, and employed the whole evening and much of the night writing letters of farewell to my numerous friends, expecting the following day would be the last I should tread on British ground. The next day, though, Mr Lyons came to tell me that there were some unavoidable delays with the vessel and I had no choice but to wait a further week. How to pass this time? Every idle hour was now a terror to me. McDougall and I resolved to take a tour to Inverary and we set off within the hour. At the top of Loch Gare we stopped off at the house of a relative of McDougall's, where we were made heartily welcome. The first ceremony was with the whisky bottle. I was in the highlands and my maxim ever was 'whilst in Rome, be the Roman' so, for the first time in my life, I topped off a glass of spirits before my morning's meal. An excellent Scotch breakfast ensued (with the addition of cheese, a mixture I had never before seen). We resumed the journey soon after, our hats during the time we were at breakfast being covered with roses, a custom prevailing on that day.

'The presence of some pretty girls was no disagreeable surprise'
We made our way on foot and by boat to the village of Lochgoilhead where the Rev McDougall, the brother of my hostess Mrs Kerr, lived. The house was charmingly situated facing the water. We arrived about four, to find dinner awaiting us on the table. The appearance of two young men I perceived created a pleasing smile upon the countenances of three or four females, a feeling I certainly shared as the presence of some pretty girls was no disagreeable surprise where only the solitary

society of an old bachelor had been expected. One of the girls, named Jessie Fleming, was on friendly terms, it transpired, with Dr Newman and his family, an astonishing co-incidence which stimulated no end of reminiscing. Another guest, a most agreeable clergyman of the name of Baylie, was on a walking tour with his daughter and the girl already mentioned and we were invited to join them on their journey to Inverary, to which we set off early the next morning. Inverary is a small neat town, with an inn lately built by the Duke of Argyle.

That evening a few of the remaining officers of the Argyle local militia who had just concluded their duty were going home, but being acquainted with McDougall they agreed to stay to initiate me into the Wallace Club, the actual cap of that hero in Liberty's cause being worn by the Chairman and preserved by the Landlord as a precious relic. I was the first Englishman that had ever been under its shade and in the initiation a long ceremony is gone through, which, however, is perfectly patriotic. The evening closed as I was informed not unusually in mirth and festivity.

The next day about 12 o'clock a boat entered the pier with our friends aboard, but they had hardly had time to mount to the steps when a most frightful commotion occurred, alarming the boatmen. We all ran to see what was afoot when, to the great terror of my friends, a huge whale came into the harbour just twenty yards away. It stuck fast on the beach, spouting water in fury from its nostrils. The ladies, in particular, were petrified, but after ten minutes or so the great beast managed to free himself and swam away. A few days were passed in leisure at Inverary with my new friends, but at last this pleasant time had to come to an end. McDougall and I took our final dinner at the inn, the ladies seated in an upstairs window watching for our departure. Many and many a farewell salute passed between us. Wishing, however, to leave them some little token, I wrote upon the back of two of my sketches which I had coloured, some appropriate words and, folding them up, sent them, directed by a cottager.

Pursued by a bull

Journeying back we were soon soaked to the skin by a torrential downpour but were determined that no impediment would stop us reaching home by nightfall. Crossing Loch Long at Ardentinny, we landed safely at the village of Letter, but by now darkness was falling. We were making our way across to the next Loch when from a farmyard the bellowing of a bull drew our attention and in another instant out rushed a very large animal, with a mouth covered with foam and seeing us instantly gave chase, ploughing up the soil as he went along. We were then about 200 yards ahead and made the best speed we could; he followed full three quarters of a mile and at last gained so upon us that we cried out to each other to separate and give him his choice. Unfortunately he took a liking to me and seeing no possible alternative of safety I dashed into the loch and waded in and held up my portfolios. He even pursued then above his knees before he stopped and, looking round for my companion, left me to my watery meditation. McDougall had contrived to secure himself behind a high wall, when the farmer with a large party came and delivered us from our perilous situation.

We crossed Loch Gare by ferry and were safely ensconced at Ardencaple Inn by 10 o'clock. Letters arrived from friends advising me that my vessel was shortly to sail and that my early embarkation was imperative.

Journey to Portugal – the voyage
Thursday 13th July
I was to sail in the brig *Anna Maria*, commanded by Captain Richer. The brig, flying a red ensign on its topmast, was standing off the port of Greenock, and by break of day with the aid of a glass I saw the vessel (whose cargo was coals and bottles) warping out of the harbour. My friends from Greenock had joined me in an early dinner and accompanied me to the beach, where I pressed my lips, perhaps for the last time, to British earth. At twenty minutes past 5 o'clock on the 13th July 1809 I embarked on board a boat at the White Faelands, a small projecting point of land between Ardencaple Inn and the village of Helensburgh on the north side of the river Clyde in Scotland and nearly facing Greenock. I was accompanied by Captain Skelton R.N., Lieutenants John McDougall of the 91st Highlanders and Archibald Galbraith. I boarded at a quarter to six and our party, shortly after joined by Lyons, drank to my success. My friends remained on board until past seven when, with a mist beginning to fall, they decided it was time to leave. After drinking a toast to our next merry meeting, they departed.

The breeze freshened from the south-west. About nine I retired to my berth which was on the larboard side of the cabin. The appearance of the cabin promised scant prospects of comfort. It was about 10 feet by six and about five in height and had recently been fumigated. I had been allotted the mate's berth and he, obliged to seek one elsewhere, had appropriated two trunks in the cabin. My sleep was too often disturbed by the rattling of the blocks and seamen running on deck to do me much service, and every four hours the whole ship was awakened by three heavy stamps from the helmsman and loud shouts of *'Larboard or Starboard watch ahoy'*.

Friday 14th July
When I arose at about eight in the morning a thick mist had formed which soon turned into a heavy shower. The vessel was then standing off Wemyss Bay in the Clyde. Six of the West India fleet passed us homeward bound. The rain fell so heavily that despite my bearskin coat I was obliged to keep below during the evening. The captain had shown strong marks of disapprobation which I was unable to fathom and during our meals I was always on the fidget. At last I was induced to ask the cause and if it lay with myself. He then told me that the mate, who ought to have taken the alternate watch with himself, had been in a state of intoxication ever since being on board. At about midnight I was woken by a tremendous noise in the cabin; this proved to be the mate who had fallen down the steps, and had I not been present to have helped him there was every chance he would have suffocated for his head was doubled under his chest. I managed to pull him to his bed like a log of wood and left him there. But scarcely had an hour passed before I saw him crawl towards his chest and take another draught from his dram bottle which I was happy to see had now done its worst injury. He kept it to his mouth sucking away long after he had drained the contents.

Saturday 15th July
The sea was considerably calmer and with a favourable wind the vessel glided rapidly through the water, the Irish coast near Belfast soon appearing on our starboard bow. The wind and weather continued favourable. At four in the evening we passed the brig *Acorn* and shortly after were brought to by a Revenue cutter. The evening was so serene that I continued walking the deck with the captain, who was on first

watch, until nearly eleven o'clock when he proposed Saturday's evening toast to 'Sweethearts and wives'. I drank it in a bumper with thoughts of the sweetest remembrances, then retired to my berth and despite all its discomforts was soon wrapped in my first sound sleep since embarkation. But at around one o'clock I was woken by the Captain shouting *'all hands upon deck and make everything snug, for we shall have it bye and bye'*. And right he was, for the wind soon increased to a gale.

Sunday 16th July
A fine breeze, Dublin Bay about three leagues distant and ten sail of vessels of various descriptions in view. I now began to find my sea legs and sea appetite for though I had not been actually sick I had nonetheless found a very unpleasant sensation creep over me. Indeed it was a lucky thing for me that my appetite was not keener for as a result of our hurried departure to beat the intended embargo the vessel had sailed with nothing but the common ship provisions on board except some poultry shipped on my account. Vinegar, salt, bread, milk, potatoes and such necessary articles were forgotten. Our breakfast usually consisted of coffee and salt meat with the hardest brown biscuits I had ever attempted to eat and which it was only possible to achieve with a good soaking. At dinner the salt beef again appeared accompanied by barley broth and a fowl. My friend Lyons had not forgotten me in the wine department, and the captain and I generally made a dead man per day but never exceeded that between us. All my dear absent friends and the 'patriots' were never forgotten in bumpers. The Captain was truly kind to me, and having often had passengers knew full well the little attentions that are necessary for their comfort. We had spent most of the evening in preparing fishing lines to employ my idle time – or rather those hours of relaxation from reading or studying which now and then occurred. Before embarkation I had been able to buy a small book entitled *The Spanish Language Rendered Easy* and a few other books which afforded me easy amusement.

That evening a little after seven we passed a pleasure boat which looked familiar. By now the Wicklow Mountains were about three leagues distant to the north-west and very shortly the blue mountains of Old England sank below the horizon. I heaved a sigh that came from an overflowing heart and with great depression of spirits went to my berth where

I lay indulging myself in pleasing yet melancholy reflections. I was soon roused from them by the most unwelcome of all visitors – bugs; our approach to the South had drawn them from their retreat, I suppose, for at least a host of them assailed me. 'One evil never comes alone' is a maxim that was fully verified, for a severe cold now affected me too.

Daylight was most anxiously looked for, and no sooner had its beams been welcomed by my waking eyes than I quitted my restless couch and had all my bed furniture brought upon deck while my berth underwent a strong scrubbing.

Monday 17th July
A fine breeze from the N.N. West soon drove us into the wide Atlantic Ocean with the Irish coast sinking fast below the horizon. About nine a square-rigged vessel hove in sight, crowding every lay of canvass she could and steering directly for us. Our captain walked the deck in some agitation and then called his mate (now somewhat more sober). *'Don't you think she's a rogue?'* he asks. *'She looks damned suspicious,'* replies the mate. *'What's to be done? Night's coming on'. 'Suppose we bear away two points to the westward'.* This was at last agreed upon and then our fears began to subside when the object of our alarm close hauled and quit us for a large ship which had appeared into view and which the captain said was a Bristol West Indian bearing up Channel.

Tuesday 18th July
The night proved a boisterous one and my slumbers were incessantly disturbed by the destruction of crockery. By Tuesday morning the floor of the cabin presented a sad spectacle of destruction, remnants of glass and pottery scattered in every direction. The weather having somewhat abated I had just turned in for a snug nap when my attention was called by the hoarse voice of the captain shouting *'Mr. Smith, quick, come on deck, there's an enemy alongside'*. In one spring I was almost there – the captain pointed to a large black fin about ten yards astern passing very slowly just above the water until it came into the shade of the vessel. For the first time I had a complete view of a shark, about seven or eight feet in length. I felt a sense of indescribable horror.

The old cock crowed his last today. He proved so sinewy that the Captain and I agreed that an additional pint of wine was required to aid digestion. Until he came to the table I was ignorant of his fate or I should certainly have interceded for a reprieve since not only were many of his seraglios more fit to die, but from the grandeur of his strut on deck he caused amusement to us all. But it emerged that the cook has received a whack from him the previous day and revenge seems an inherent human passion.

Wednesday 19th July
The Captain turned in about 8 o'clock, and, seeing me, said, *'Sir, you are now in the Bay of Biscay'*. We were under close reefed topsails and the sea was rolling mountains high. It put me in mind of the old ballad of the Bay of Biscay, for surely enough there we lay all day rolling our gunnels with every lurch.

Thursday 20th July
The wind continued from the eastward. About 11 o'clock we passed an American bound for Falmouth which at first sighting had caused the captain some anxiety, so much so in fact that I had gone quickly down to my cabin convinced that we would soon be steering a very different tack towards France, and I had therefore secured a few gold sovereigns in my cravat. Later the wind became colder. I produced the few cigars which I had received from my friend Lean. The captain and I puffed away together before deciding that such good cigars deserved to be accompanied by a drink. In a bumper we drank the health of the girl we loved best. With sweet thoughts of Ann I slept well that night.

Friday 21st July
By eight in the morning the shark was back. Is it in the power of such a creature to divine the secrets of nature as to foresee our fortune? It really seems so as for several days he had not been seen, but this morning he appeared particularly on the alert, the more so as the storm increased. By about midday it rose to hurricane level. One wave washed completely over us and although the sailors escaped a large Newfoundland dog was carried overboard. In a few minutes he screamed and disappeared. The tail of the shark soon showed but no vestige of the dog was to be seen. About ten minutes later, though, as if in triumph, the shark leaped from the water.

Saturday 22nd July
Misery, misery, I passed a wretched night, our approach to the south having brought out bugs once more in their thousands. The captain said he should scarcely have known my face it was so distorted. I must recount a very singular event. On the first day after we had lost sight of land two butterflies were observed repeatedly flying around the vessel despite by then being nearly 200 miles from any land. Before leaving Scotland I had exchanged my drab jacket with Lt McDougall for a green tartan one. As I made my appearance on deck the butterflies instantly recognised my green, fluttered around me and fixed on my arms where they remained for hours as I walked the deck. This they did daily as long as they were with us which was until the 24th, when we concluded that a tremendous gale had blown them away. We toasted all bumpers to sweethearts and wives and I retired to my berth with sweet prepossessions.

Sunday 23rd July
A thick mist was falling. About ten o'clock a dreadful rolling sea met us from the bay and with each roll the gunnels were under water. Not having experienced any seasickness I boldly faced the elements and took my accustomed daily walk for two hours. The weather had been so hazy for the past two days that it had prevented any observations being taken, so a strict watch was kept for land. The night was boisterous, the sea perpetually breaking over the deck, and the captain when he returned from his midnight watch was wet to the skin.

Monday 24th July
With yet another cloudy day preventing observations being taken the captain, knowing land could not be far away, became very uneasy. About 2 o'clock the wind increased so much and so suddenly as to call him from his dinner upon deck. The lurch of the vessel exceeded all I had experienced. In an instant, with a tremendous oath, all hands were called from below. A dreadful confusion ensued. *'Ease off the foretop gallant sheets, let go the top gallant halyards,'* shouted the Captain. *'Quick my hearties or we'll lose the foretop mast.'* *'Aye, aye,'* says an old veteran, but he was too slow to prevent the catastrophe and the foretop mast went with a tremendous crash. In an instant I was upon deck where I could only keep my legs with great difficulty. The captain was beside himself

and ran backwards and forwards shouting *'Ease off the main top sheet, lower the peak or by God all's gone.'* The hull of the vessel was buried in surf. He turned round, seeing me upon deck. *'You had better go below Sir.'* 'Pshaw,' said I. *'Then for God's sake take hold of something.'* I took good care to do so. Two reefs were taken in, the main topsail and the foresail which with a foretop mast staysail was all the canvas we could carry. The sea rolled in awful grandeur and the captain felt greatly uneasy, apprehensive that the coast of Portugal was on our lee. Heavy rain obscured it, and, of course, no observations of our latitude had been possible for several days.

Tuesday 25th July
The weather cleared up and a double portion of grog was promised to the first man who sighted land. The mast head was often climbed to but it was not until nearly 2 o'clock that happy information was hollered out. A heavy swell continued after the gales of the last two days and we were carried fast in towards land. By seven we were about five leagues from the coast.

Wednesday 26th July
Land lay about two leagues on our lee bow. The captain being ignorant of the appearance of Oporto was guided solely by an old man of war's sailor who said he had been there. A large bay appeared which the Captain stood off and on for several tacks with a signal for a pilot. A chart was referred to in order to see if it was a clear coast, and, since it appeared to be so and with sufficient depth of water, we went boldly in until about a mile from land. A boat was at last seen labouring to us through very heavy surf and with the crew making signals to us with their hats, but not comprehending we stayed on our course. As they neared us we could hear them speaking very loud. The captain now thought not all was right and stopped the vessel's course. Our visitors then came on deck and tremendous confusion ensued since neither country could understand the other. But from their calling out Vigo and pointing to land I told the captain that I thought he must have mistaken the place for Oporto. I brought the chart on deck and pointed out Vigo to the man at the helm. He replied *'Si, Si'*, and, first putting his finger on shoals and rocks laid down in the map, then pointed left and right of the vessel.

The captain became alarmed, and indeed it was a miracle we had not been dashed to atoms. The pilot, having put the vessel about and steered us clear of the coast, left us. We now stood down, and with a stiff breeze we followed a course about two leagues from shore, passing the ports of Baiona and Viana. I made a sketch of Viana which was made picturesque from the accompaniment of several boats of peculiar construction with preposterously large square sails.

In the evening we passed within sight of the Vila do Conde which is rendered conspicuous by an immense pile of buildings on the shore, a convent called 'Santa Clara', the inhabitants of which had suffered dreadful brutality from the French after they had captured Oporto. The greater part of the coast was covered with buildings behind which rose towering hills of broken, craggy rock. With a thick mist coming on about 8 o'clock the Captain stood off and on, concerned he must be nearing Oporto, the coast of which is covered with rocks far out to sea.

Chapter 3

Portugal

EDITORS' NOTE

Spanish Prelude: Corunna, January 1809
'Not a drum was heard...'

The wind, blowing hard from the south-west, plucked at the young clergyman's vestments. Henry Symons, Chaplain to the Brigade of Guards, had been instructed to keep the burial service short. The previous evening he had attended Sir John Moore in his last moments. It was now around eight in the morning of the 7th January, and the French guns had begun firing at the ships in the harbour below. The small group of officers might be called away at any moment, so it was necessary that the general be buried with the minimum of delay. After his death the previous evening his body had been carried to the citadel. Since he had frequently stated that should he die in battle he wanted to be buried where he had fallen it had been decided not to return his remains for burial in England. He was to be buried on the ramparts. No coffin had been obtainable, so the general was buried in his cloak, his body lowered into the hastily dug grave on the sashes of the four officers present.[1]

Over the previous days the retreat from Salamanca across the mountains of Galicia to the coast had been carried out in dreadful conditions. Demoralised by having to retreat, the army had suffered badly. They were hopelessly outnumbered, and had been harried all the way by Marshall Soult's forces. But problems arose less from the French pursuit than from appalling weather and semi-starvation caused by supply shortages.[2] Discipline had gradually broken down, yet the British army had put up a fierce resistance, especially at Elvinas, and it was here that Sir John Moore had been wounded. The brave defence, and Soult's delayed final assault, had enabled the evacuation of most of the survivors, many of them on the night of Moore's death. The transports that were to carry them back to England lay in the harbour at Corunna, under fire from the French guns, as the short funeral service concluded.

British commitment to Portugal

After Corunna there had been widespread disillusion in Britain with Spain: the collapse of the Spanish armies that had necessitated Moore's retreat was a major element in this together with numerous reports of Spanish callousness to British troops, but there were other tensions, including the extravagance of Spanish demands for aid and resentment over refusals to grant British merchants access to Spain's American colonies.[3] Moreover, the dreadful state of the survivors when they landed in England had shocked those who had seen them. Should Britain abandon the Iberian Peninsula? Many thought so. Napoleon's forces held sway over much of Europe, and by early 1809 they were certainly well entrenched in Spain.

There were, however, some influential voices advocating support for Portugal. Prominent among them was Sir Arthur Wellesley who argued that Portugal alone offered the prospect of maintaining a British land presence on the continent. Wellesley had been in Portugal, fought there and was convinced it could be held. British forces would have the sea at their backs offering direct and secure lines of communication and supply. The country favoured a defensive army: hills, ravines and broken ground with few open plains on which the French could deploy their cavalry. Moreover, British troops would be fighting in a friendly country in which it would be easy to get information as well as mules and muleteers for supplies. Portuguese soldiers were potentially valuable allies, although much would depend on reforming and rebuilding an effective army. By contrast, whatever the numerical superiority and experience of the French army, they would have long lines of communication across the hostile country of Spain and Portugal. George Canning, the Foreign Secretary, was persuaded, and he had been a decisive influence in securing Britain's commitment to Portugal and in getting Wellesley appointed to command the British army.[4]

Sir Arthur Wellesley arrived in Portugal on the 22nd April. French forces were in control of Oporto and had been since Soult had captured the town on 28th March. But Wellesley's forces, in a brilliant operation, were able to dislodge Soult on 12th May and had then pursued his army north. British commanders had hoped to encircle the retreating army and destroy it but after making daring assaults French forces had been able to secure and cross vital bridges, the British having to be content with mauling a small rearguard. Nevertheless, even if they had not eliminated Soult's army the British had inflicted heavy casualties while only suffering light losses themselves. Soult's forces lost all their artillery, virtually all their heavy baggage, and were driven from Portugal.

* * *

My arrival in Oporto: 'a swarm of harpies'

On Thursday the 27th we stood in towards land. By the time I arose, about six o'clock, we could, with the use of a glass, plainly make out a large fort, and by nine we were near enough to see people walking on shore. A gun was fired from the fort and then a large red ensign hoisted to tell us the bar was impassable. Eventually, around midday, a pilot came out to the ship. We were guided back over the bar, a tremendous sandbank which stretched right across the river. There was always a large swell over it and a skilful helmsman was needed to navigate it. First land was made at São João da Foz near the mouth of the Douro. Here you undergo the first ordeal of the Custom House, a swarm of whose harpies tear you almost to pieces in begging provisions – it was hardly credible but many really well dressed persons asked charity of cheese, etc.

Having received an initial bill of health the pilot escorted our brig up the Douro towards Oporto, about 2½ miles upstream. As we approached the town the views grew increasingly impressive. On both sides of the river the banks rose steeply, covered with buildings, most with balconies, and interspersed with beautiful hanging gardens of orangeries and vine walks. After sailing up about a mile to a bay, the river, thronged with traffic, formed an angle, and here Oporto burst into view. Houses clamber up the steep riverbank. No two houses are alike and the dwelling of even the meanest merchant has its veranda. The ground floors near the river are not usually lived in: they might be shops, form passages or be used as stables or coach houses. The verandas are heavy in appearance, mainly of wood and painted dark red.

The ship now endured a second visit from the Customs House. Ships were brought to an anchor in mid-river, forming a sort of quarantine. Then two ill-looking vagabonds calling themselves 'guards' brought their bed and bedding with them on board the vessel and to my no small mortification I learnt I must not go on shore without a custom house clearance. I confess I was much disappointed and was not sparing of my abuse (not reflecting they neither understood me nor were to blame). When I retired to rest I found one of these worthy persons *sans ceremonie* had taken possession of my berth having just removed my bed furniture. John Bull must not suffer an insult from a Portuguese and therefore, having with much civility explained to him that I had paid for that berth, with a most significant shrug he returned *'Non intende Signor'*. He was preparing to lie down when I found myself reluctantly compelled to use a language he must understand and, seizing his legs, soon exposed his pretty person upon the floor and calling down two of the sailors (who by the by enjoyed the joke highly) had all my bedding restored to its former situation.

At last, around midday, I was able to leave the ship. Almost as soon as I landed I approached a British officer[5] who recommended a hotel. Once I found a room I settled down to write a long letter home to report my safe arrival. Closer inspection of the town proved deeply disappointing: the ideas I had formed from the river of the grandeur and style of Oporto instantly evaporated. The streets were narrow, unpaved and filthy. But what struck me most forcibly was the noise: the Portuguese speak so excessively loud and so many at the same time, accompanied with great action with feet as well as hand, that they convey the idea of madmen – added to which your ears are dreadfully annoyed by the grating of the wheels of the carts, which convey the merchandise of the town – 12 or 14 of which often follow in succession and produce all the tones of the gamut – but in horrid discord. Indeed, the annoyance was so great that the Governor was obliged to compel the use of grease under a severe penalty. These were drawn by oxen, horses and mules being used only for saddle or for drawing carriages. These *caliches* are at least a century behind those used in England in comfort and appearance: they carry only two people and are open at the front with only leather curtains to give protection against wet or very hot weather.

'The delicate feelings of the Englishman'

The close trading contacts between Britain and Portugal are evidenced in the clothing of the younger merchants, which would not have been out of place on the streets of Bristol. For older men it was a different story, for they have every appearance of quack doctors dressed in all the gaudy colours of a macaw. Most men wear large cocked hats crowned by a patriotic cockade while the fashion of the better-off women mirrors British styles. The peasantry wear brightly-coloured waistcoats, heavily embroidered and ornamented with buttons and with immense bundles of petticoats suspended from them. Numerous trinkets and ornaments adorned bosoms, ears and fingers. But a most filthy custom of lousing each other prevails so generally that the delicate feelings of the Englishman is hurt whichever way he looks, scarcely five yards in the streets are free from the subject – and instead of performing the duty as a task it affords to the Portuguese a pleasing recreation. Indeed the criterion of friendship between the fair sex is to louse each other, but the practice is more particularly offensive in the markets, when in the midst of meat, fruit and vegetables you see it – and as every stall has in general two or more persons, all the time unoccupied in vending their goods is devoted to this pleasing recreation and the very nail perhaps in which the death blow has been given is the next moment, uncleaned, touching the article about to be purchased.

Although the setting of Oporto, high above and sloping down to the Douro, is imposing, and there are many handsome individual casas, much of the town to my eye is unimpressive. There are few good streets, and all are badly paved. At night lights are scarce, and the few that can be found shed a glimmering light on figures of Our Lord. These are set on the walls of houses and are dressed up in a tawdry style that reminded me of nothing so much as toys to amuse children at an English fair. Darkness brings its own hazards: the cowardly custom of back assassination which prevails in so much of the country from the great want of lights during the nights might be committed in Oporto without the fear of detection. Although it has been said to be on the decline two incidents occurred in the short time I was in the city and neither excited much alarm or effort to find the perpetrators. The town has no police or guard at night apart from the military town guard. There seems a natural disposition to idleness, and poverty is considered a lesser evil than labour. Nature might bless Portugal with a good climate but their sluggish disposition subjects the inhabitants to want, filth and wretchedness. Much of the country is uncultivated and except where there are woods or vineyards much of the land is burnt up, sandy and pestilential. The streets of Oporto swarm with monks of various orders, but their reign of terror is on the decline, as much of their wanted respect is now refused them. Indeed the visit of the French, though accompanied with every suffering of rapine, murder and plunder, yet has not been without its salutary effect: many of the monasteries are cleared of their useless occupants and whole fraternities of those lazy drones turned adrift and their convents appropriated for barracks which practice has been since followed by the English.

Portuguese women are generally small with dark features. They gesture freely in conversation which at least has the advantage of making them understood by the English, very few of whom have made any progress with the language. When alone in the street most women cover themselves with a large black cloak and expose little of their faces. The men are often handsome and fine-limbed, and are reported to be brave soldiers in the field when headed by foreign officers (Portuguese officers lacking confidence in either the skill or bravery of their own). There is excessive intimacy and familiarity between officers and men which undermines respect and discipline, one of the causes of which may be poor pay, for junior officers are, I am told, paid little more than an English corporal. The introduction of British officers into the Portuguese army is having beneficial effects although exciting considerable jealousy. Portuguese troops are shoddily turned out and so badly uniformed that even Falstaff's motley associates would have seemed smart by comparison.

One effect of foreign armies, both British and French, had been to reduce national jealousies between Portugal and Spain. The French had behaved with unspeakable savagery. Over the course of three days 30,000 troops had run riot in Oporto, committing every sort of enormity, particularly in the nunneries where they had treated the nuns with great brutality. The cruelties of the French were fresh in the minds of the Oportans. Murders had been commonplace, women and girls raped, sometimes on the dead or dying body of any husband or father who had offered resistance. Now the Portuguese had had the chance of retaliation, and by all accounts had refined cruelty and perfected methods of delivering a lingering death.

The Battle of Oporto
During my time in Oporto I got to know Captain Isaac L'Estrange well. L'Estrange was with the 3rd Foot (Buffs) which had played a central part in the British victory in Oporto on 12th May. He took me across the

battlefield, pointing out places where British troops had acted with great bravery. He passed modestly over his own role, though I was later to learn that his bravery was conspicuous and his escape miraculous. He had had one particularly narrow escape when while drinking from the canteen of one of his soldiers, an enemy rifleman had aimed at him only for the bullet to pass through the body of the soldier and strike the canteen in his hand. The poor fellow had dropped without a sound into the arms of a comrade.

L'Estrange described the course of events that day. On the 11th May the two armies had been closely engaged and the French forced to withdraw towards Grijó. At daybreak the British army found the French had crossed to the north bank of the Douro and made good their retreat to Oporto. To frustrate the British advance Soult had destroyed the Bridge of Boats and also brought all other boats over to the north bank. According to L'Estrange's account Sir Arthur Wellesley had command of about 15,000 British troops.[6] Wellesley immediately established an observation post from the Monastery da Sera do Pilar, set high on the south bank and giving clear views of Oporto across the river. The left wing of the Buffs was ordered to proceed about half a mile upstream just beyond an abrupt bend in the river which masked them from observation. It was near here that three boats were discovered which had escaped the attention of the French.[7] The Buffs were the first to embark. The crossing continued steadily with the 48th (Northamptonshires) and the 66th (Berkshires) reinforcing the Buffs, and later by other units which included the 60th, a rifle brigade, and some cavalry. The first instructions had been to scale the steep route to a seminary which had been left unoccupied and unguarded; a long three-storey building in a prominent position above the town, this made an ideal bastion for the British forces. By the time the French discovered what was happening about five or six companies of British forces were firmly lodged in the seminary. A considerable number of French cavalry were then seen approaching but in poor formation. A further force of some 2000 French infantry advanced on the seminary, keeping in close formation and maintaining incessant but irregular fire. The British forces were outnumbered but had excellent cover from the building and using this they were able to inflict heavy casualties on the French and to force a retreat.[8] With more of the Buffs arriving from across the river and reinforced by the 48th and 66th the

View of Oporto near Mosteiro da Serra de Pilar from where Wellington conducted the Battle of Oporto in May 1809

defenders moved onto the offensive, rushing out into the gardens and shrubberies of the suburbs. Heavy firing continued. The British were facing experienced troops from the celebrated 70th, or Invincibles, men who had seen action in Egypt with Bonaparte, at Maida with Regnier and at Vimiero before coming under Soult's command at Corunna. The action was maintained for an hour until three in the afternoon when the French retreated up a long avenue of cork trees. The trees were soon shattered, perforated by bullets from all sides. It was here that the soldier had been killed while L'Estrange drank from his canteen. At the end of the walk was a high and richly ornamented gate bounded by high walls, storming which cost many British lives. About 1,600 French were positioned on the outside, formed in open columns, and as they passed the gate they wheeled up, fired and quickly moved on, only exposing themselves in the act of firing. The British initially used the trees as cover before eventually forcing the gate. Around three hundred of the enemy lay dead or wounded at the gate, and a number of Portuguese died from exercising their curiosity too close to the action. Meanwhile a large French detachment moved to the right and attempted unsuccessfully to force two substantial houses in which the 48th and 66th had installed themselves. Total French forces engaged in these actions numbered around 6000, almost three times the British numbers. The remainder, under Soult, made good their retreat. It was at this stage that the Portuguese took revenge. As the British moved on in quick pursuit of the retreating army they left behind wounded French soldiers where they fell. The local inhabitants, armed with every instrument of assassination, moved in. Seizing on the wounded they tormented them to a death which, though certain ultimately, was delayed for the purpose of torture with every species of brutality. Many, seeing the fate of their comrades, seized the legs of the British as they moved over them, imploring them with heart-piercing shrieks in the voice of humanity to be protected from the Portuguese.

L'Estrange estimated that about 100 British troops had been killed against French losses of 800, including prisoners, as well as five pieces of ordinance.[9] The British did not attempt to follow up their victory, and many blamed Wellesley, alleging that a complete defeat of the enemy could have been achieved. But such persons do not take into account its practicability. The British troops had been on the move for several days and had suffered many hardships and privations. Rest was imperative.[10] I cannot help mentioning a circumstance showing the ingratitude of the people of Oporto. The city had been cleared of its oppressors and prayers had been answered. But when a request was made to the Chief Magistrate for wine for the troops, a request detailing their hardships and deprivation, it was refused unless personal security for payment was given. When told of this Sir Arthur peremptorily declared that unless his request was immediately met he would march his troops into the factory cellars. Wine eventually appeared but not before the troops had endured a long wait in hot and sultry weather.

When viewed from the river the setting of the town is very picturesque, the height of the banks lending it grandeur. I sketched the scene, taking a viewpoint just below the Bridge of Boats. In the distance to the left is the unfinished seminary which had played such a crucial role in the British assault, to the right Vila Nova from where a small path winds up to the Monastery Serra do Pilar. Both to the front and at the rear of the building are beautiful hanging gardens and shrubberies, from where Wellesley had planned and overseen the attack. On the left is part of Oporto: a gate leads to the Customs House. Beyond is part of the old city walls built in the Moorish style. Constructed high above the river on steep rocks the town would have been impregnable were it not vulnerable from the opposite bank. At the top is the Convent of St. Clara. Wine barges are in the foreground together with one of many hundred ferry boats.

'A bloody washing'

I decided to move from the oppressive atmosphere of Oporto and on the 8th August moved to the small town of São João da Foz, renowned for its bathing, where I obtained a good billet. There is a fort at the mouth of the river which looks formidable but would not be able to hold out against a frigate if it could approach with safety, though for much of the year large ships have great difficulty in getting anywhere near the fort. The notoriously dangerous bank extends almost completely across the entrance to the river, and in winter particularly the sea rolls across the bar with irresistible violence, sometimes making it impassable for months at a time.

The dangers of the sandbank were distressingly revealed only a few days after I arrived in São João da Foz When vessels approach the bar guns are fired from the fort to warn them if passage is too dangerous. At about seven on the evening of Friday 11th August a gun from the fort was fired. This aroused little curiosity at first until crowds started to run towards the beach. I followed and, arriving there, saw a small boat with five people aboard, about a quarter mile from the shore, engulfed by breakers. As the boat continued to struggle against the conditions the dangers increased. The awful scene was heightened by the repeated firing of the warning gun from the fort. A local crew launched a pilot skiff in a bold attempt at rescue, but a huge wave came towards the small boat and the worst fears of the spectators were realised. The boat, overwhelmed, went down, and for half a minute was lost to view. When it re-surfaced four of the crew were seen clinging to its sides. The pilot skiff battled through the sea in repeated attempts to reach the vessel but it was too dangerous to get closer than 100 yards. As night began to fall remaining hope for the crew faded: the seas worsened, and the boat often disappeared from view in a sea of white foam. Spectators nearest the water knelt in prayer. In the growing dark, in case any attempted to swim ashore, a hawthorn was suspended from a pole to indicate the best part of the beach for a safe landing, avoiding the hazardous rocks that hemmed them in. Later, at about nine, one of the crew was picked up, still clinging to the floating boat but nearly exhausted and with life scarcely perceptible. He was however no sooner landed on terra firma than truly characteristic of his profession and no longer thinking of danger, he exclaimed: *'Damn my eyes, but I have had a bloody washing'*. He was carried up to the house where I was staying, rubbed down well and various remedies applied. The boat belonged to the Syrian gun brig. One of the men, a powerful swimmer, had stripped and, trusting to his skills, had left his shipmates. Not long afterwards two of the others were washed off by a huge wave, the crewman just rescued remaining alone in the boat. At about eleven the two who had been washed overboard were also picked up: after surfacing they had managed to seize on to two oars and were floating on these when found. The swimmer was never heard of again.

Voyage to Lisbon: the naked and the dead

I received my first news from England a week later and I was instructed to move to Lisbon. I managed to secure a passage on one of two transports taking sick and wounded British troops from Oporto to the capital and, together with Captain L'Estrange, I embarked on Monday morning, the 21st August. On board were two wounded officers and about 80 men. We had trouble leaving the port for by about 8 o'clock the transport was drifting near the bar with little wind and strong currents that alarmed both captain and pilot. But we were soon in open sea under full sail and escorted in convoy by the mighty frigate HMS *Semiramis*, commanded by Captain William Grainger.

Around ten o'clock one of the sick (a man of the Buffs and well-known to L'Estrange) died of dysentery. An hour later he was brought on deck, sewn up in his blanket and committed to the sea. All this took place amongst the jokes and laughter of the crew, many of whom had been his comrades in battle and others that, judging from their wretched appearance, had scarcely a hope of any better fate. Man is soon taught to laugh at the grimmest of events once inured to misery.

We sailed on in high but favourable winds until, around midnight, a gunshot from the frigate produced confusion on deck and woke the whole ship. A second shot was followed by signals from the Commodore. Before the captain had time to consult his book of signals a third shot sung overhead. The Captain swore violently and then shouted *'We are upon Berlangas'* (a dangerous shoal of rocks off Peniche): *'Ease off sheets, let go fore top halyards and helm hard up'*. Amidst the turmoil on deck everyone looked to their own preservation. The horror of the scene was much heightened by the exertions of the poor unfortunate wounded fellows, who were seen crawling from the hold – some in their shirts, others naked, with mutilated persons, that conveyed a strong resemblance to that day 'when the grave shall open and give forth its dead'. The hand of Providence was with us, for it appeared beyond the power of human effort to avert our danger. A temporary lull of the wind gave time for the necessary shifting of the sails and we had the gratifying intelligence of 'All's Well'.

Some returned to their berths while those who felt strong enough remained on deck all night. Favourable winds continued and at around eight next morning allowed the captain to approach the coast. We hugged the undulating coast for the remainder of the voyage until at last the Rock of Lisbon came into view. About two miles inland, dark grey and rugged, it is topped at one of the highest points by a celebrated convent. From here along to Lisbon lie a chain of strong fortifications, one of which, the Cascaes fort, five miles from the mouth of the Tagus, requires a garrison of about 1800 men. This was to have been stormed by the Buffs had not the Battle of Vimiero and consequent convention made it unnecessary. Further towards Lisbon is a smaller fort, Il Antonio. The entrance to the Tagus is commanded by Il Julien and by Bugio, a small insulated fort. Il Julien, which extends to the water's edge, covers a large area. The French occupied it, I had heard, with only 1200 men but because of its size at least 4000 would have been needed in the event of a siege. There were, however, doubts over the ability of Il Julieno to withstand a long siege because a small hill runs gradually from the fort and at a quarter of a mile's distance is parallel in height with the fortifications. The French had intended either to blow up the hill, difficult to achieve because of the hardness of the rock, or, therefore more probably, have constructed an advanced redoubt on the summit.

Lisbon would have been very difficult to attack from the sea as at its entrance the Tagus is about four miles wide and guarded by two well placed forts. But if hostile ships did succeed in getting past the first forts they would have encountered further trouble ten miles up the river where

Belem Tower

it narrowed to about two miles. Here there were two further forts, on the north bank the superbly constructed castle of Belem and on the south the small fortification of Fouval. The base of the Belem fort consists largely of a single arched apartment, about seven feet high, with ten or twelve small embrasures for cannons which from their position could do a great deal of mischief. The only entrance is a small door close to the water's edge and within this is a low arched gateway with a portcullis grate which leads down to the lower apartment. A straight narrow flight of steps leads up to the first suite of apartments; these might effectively be defended by ten men against an attack by a thousand. On this lodgement are soldiers' barracks, a large prison and a platform on three sides of the building where there are a further twelve cannon. A circular flight of steps, about ninety, leads to the top of the building. Several apartments branch off from the steps and a passage leads out to a small parapet for musketry on one side of which battlements are formed in the shape of shields and from which fire can be directed against assailants under the wall. The building is richly ornamented with carving and enhanced by the round watch towers at the corners.

Belem is a town in itself, and, as it is so near the sea, popular in summer, the King of Portugal and many of the nobility having palaces there. The British ambassador, John Villiers, occupies the Patriarch's very large though uncompleted palace. The famous convent, founded by Alphonse Henrique in 1145, is situated here also. Dedicated to the Virgin Mary, it is home to a fraternity of nearly 30 Benedictines. The entrance to the church, built from marble which has over time become dark red, is as fine a piece of carving as any in Portugal. The building is a mixture of Gothic and Moorish (or Arabesque Gothic) styles, the extreme elegance and lightness of the latter combining with the strength and solidity of the former.

From the great hall, where there is a collection of miserably bad paintings of the crowned heads of Portugal, a door opens into a gallery, fully four hundred feet long, on either side of which are small doors opening into the cells of the brothers. Over each of these is a Latin superscription to remind its occupant of futurity and of how passing and unfruitful a nature are all engagements of this transitory life. The cloisters are of the same style as the church and very ornamented. Some of the arches are semicircular and diverge from the obtuse and the sharp pointed Gothic and in the centre is a garden with pools with numerous fish. Within this again, approached by four stone causeways, is a small square island filled with fragrant herbs and plants laid out in a formal style typical of Italian gardens.

Chapter 4

Lisbon and the Road to Elvas

Lisbon
The road from Belem slips almost imperceptibly into Lisbon, three or four miles distant: there is no clear boundary between the towns. The capital had suffered massive destruction on 1st November 1755 when up to one-third of the population had died during the earthquakes and the fires that followed. Such was the scale of devastation that there had been a strong move to relocate the court and seat of government to Oporto but the Marquis of Pombal had persuaded the king to remain in Lisbon and to take the opportunity to rebuild and transform the city, and much of its present splendour is due to the exertions of the Marquis.

Lisbon, like ancient Rome, is built upon several hills, and in extent must exceed Oporto at least four times. At its centre the land is level, and it was here that much of the worst of the destruction had been concentrated, the collapse of St Nicholas Church alone killing hundreds who had been attending Mass on All Souls' Day. Of the monarch's palace, scarcely a vestige remained after the earthquake. The Marquis oversaw the rebirth of the city and he was responsible for the design of many of the buildings that emerged from the rubble of the old centre. A large square, the Praça do Comércio, faces on to the river. At its centre is a stupendous equestrian bronze statue of one of the kings in Roman costume. Marshall Junot had intended to relocate this to Paris and had actually commenced removing the palisade when the Convention of Vimiero was signed. Junot's action was frustrated when Sir Arthur Wellesley sent his Aide de Camp to point out that this would be a direct breach of the convention.

The town centre is built with the greatest uniformity. Lisbon might be made one of the cleanest of cities, instead of which dirt and filth of every description reign pre-eminently.[1] Except in the *casas* of the higher classes of society a certain convenience called a 'necessary' is not to be met with. In its stead large jars made of clay about three-quarters of a yard high are substituted. As soon as dusk sets in the contents of these are hurled *sans ceremonie* out of the windows without warning. The destruction of the windows by the English troops has however had the good effect of creating a little respect when a red coat is near. The only scavengers to cleanse away this filth are dogs which are nearly as numerous as the inhabitants and who, subject to no master, range through the town without control. But for them plague or pestilence would make Lisbon their seat of government; for rather than take a little trouble the Portuguese will endure the greatest violence to their nerves.

First setback: interview with Marshall Beresford

L'Estrange and I landed in Lisbon on 22nd August and found rooms at the Latours Hotel in the Praça dos Romulares, a small square facing the river. I had a full view of the river and its shipping from my bed. And from there I counted 160 ships, most of a distinctive design but well-equipped to weather a heavy sea. Next day, following instructions, I collected a large packet of letters from Majes Power and Co. in Rua da Emenda. Many of these were letters of introduction which friends at home had supplied for me to present to senior military officers in the Peninsula. These were the key to my plan to join the army and I now set about delivering as many of them as possible. The ship carrying my regimentals had not yet arrived, so I spent the next few days attempting to make arrangement for my future.

One letter was to Brigadier-General George Madden who had just arrived in Lisbon with an appointment to the Portuguese Army.[2] I waited upon him and was most kindly received and through his interest had a long interview with Marshal William Beresford. The Portuguese government had requested London to send a British officer to take command of their army and Beresford had been sent with the task of turning the army into an effective fighting force.[3] His advice to me was given with every appearance of sincerity, and he pointed out the drawbacks of the Portuguese army. Not least of these was the difficulty of obtaining a commission. Horse Guards had refused to sanction ranks promised to British officers even though they had already been serving for several months. I would have had no chance, and even if I had been fortunate enough to achieve a good rank I could of course lose all in a moment by enemy action.

Seeing my hopes thus blasted in that quarter I was left with no recourse but the British Army, and to that the Marshal urged me to go. Losses

William Carr Beresford, Viscount Beresford by Sir William Beechey 'His advice was given with every appearance of sincerity.' © National Portrait Gallery, London

among British officers at the Battle of Talavera a month earlier had been high, and the Marshal thought I would have every chance of success. Sir Arthur was then retreating from Spain to Elvas, a strongly fortified town to the east of Lisbon and just inside the Portuguese border.

Finding myself compelled to wait in Lisbon until my trunks arrived, I devoted my time to viewing the town and drawing. What impressed me most was the aqueduct that supplied water to Lisbon over a nine-mile course. Its most spectacular section was the point where it crosses a deep ravine about a mile outside the city where it stood over 200 feet above the river. I noted down the Latin inscription in my journal.[4]

While I was admiring this most magnificent work my attention was excited by a mob of about fifty men passing by, guarded by a small posse of cavalry. Several bad-looking fellows were bolted together and, on asking what crimes had they committed, I was astonished to be told they were volunteers, or patriots, on their way to the army. How can the least hope of ultimate success exist in the cause of liberty when its first vital principle is thus crushed? Can a particle of the fire of freedom exist in minds thus debased by the shackles of slavery? No! Yet on this conscription the Portuguese build their hopes of emancipation.

Mula

Finding my prospects thwarted in respect of the Portuguese army I now had to make preparations for the journey to Elvas. One vital part of this was to buy a mule, and with this in mind I visited various markets. All the old campaigners advised strongly that paying a high price was ultimately the least expensive option. But prospective purchasers far outnumbered vendors and prices ran high. I was offered several wretched-looking creatures for between a hundred and a hundred and ten dollars, none of which I was convinced could have borne the rigours of a journey to the Spanish border. Various accounts had reached me of officers whose mules had dropped miles from human habitation and who had been forced to remain with their baggage until some humane muleteer passed by and gave assistance. Finding nothing in the Lisbon markets, I headed towards Belem where, I had been told, officers on their way back to England would readily dispose of their livestock. My timing was poor: the arrival of the 1st Royals had nearly doubled the price. I was on my return to Lisbon, completely exhausted by my walk and despondent from my ill-success when my fortunes changed. I chanced to meet an old acquaintance from England to whom I had rendered assistance in the past, Lieutenant John Blundell of the Fusiliers. Having apprised him of my situation, Blundell introduced me to a particular friend of his, Captain Fry, who had been wounded and was returning to England. Fry possessed a small but handsome mule, and, with a promise of good usage from me, we soon closed on a price of 140 dollars. Since this included a good saddle and bridle it was a cheap price, and, indeed, scarcely ten minutes had passed before I was offered 160 dollars for the mule, an offer I readily refused.

Except in the streets dominated by particular trades almost every fourth shop is converted into a coffee house – a *Casa de Café* – almost all of which were sumptuously decorated. The tables are mostly marble slabs. These cafés are popular with the Portuguese for smoking and drinking coffee but their habit of smoking before breakfast greatly offends English noses. The Lisbon theatres are generally regarded as poor, most of the better actors having left when the French arrived in the city. I attended the opera but there was only one good female singer, the dancing was inferior and the scenery wretched. The building, about the same size as the new Bath theatre, is impressive, particularly the elaborately decorated Royal Box; this is rarely used now but had always been occupied by Junot when he attended. The night I went happened to be on the anniversary of the entry of the British into Lisbon after the Battle of Vimiero, and a humble representation of it was introduced into the ballet.

Lisbon is entirely under the protection of the military who act as its police. There are two or three corps of volunteers, raised in the city, who make a very presentable appearance, especially the Merchants Corps. Not the least notable features are their whiskers and moustaches which they are permitted to grow to a preposterous size. The patriots are mounted and parade the city and its suburbs day and night.

Journey to Elvas
Friday 22nd September
I began my journey to the army on Friday 22nd September, travelling with Lieutenant Peter McArthur of the Buffs who had just arrived in Lisbon after a long convalescence following the retreat to Corunna, and who was now set on rejoining his regiment. He willingly accepted my offer of the mule for carrying our mutual baggage, and we were accompanied by a soldier. At ten we set out equipped with a haversack, canteens holding two quarts, a spy glass and my portfolio. Our route to the army, which lay in cantonments around Elvas and just across the border near Badajos, took us across the Tagus to Aldea Galleja. Despite a favourable wind the crossing took us about two hours, the river here being nearly twelve miles wide.

The town was thronged with military going to and coming from the army. Our first task was to find a billet for the night. The allocation of billets to officers is usually the responsibility of a species of mayor, generally the most reputable person in the town or village. In practice the job is in the hands of a deputy, the *Juiz da Fora*, often likely to be an ignorant fellow whose joy is to keep the epaulets waiting and to extract as much information about the army as possible. It was therefore nearly three o'clock before we found accommodation.

Finally we were ushered upstairs to a very decent apartment and at once divested ourselves of our equipment. We were soon joined by a small man who by appearance and his immense strides quickly established that he was the landlord and not pleased to see us. Since the room was only about twelve feet long he was only permitted about three strides in each direction. My friend and self, occupying the sofa, paid but little attention to his rage: the words 'Jacobin' and 'revenge' were repeated and seemed to refer to the *Juiz*'s deputy. Before long the mistress of the house appeared, a short, copper-coloured woman who took her seat and apologised for her hot-headed nephew. The size of the beauteous Senhora exceeded all I had ever seen – from the extreme edge of her bosom the fall to her feet was perpendicular.

Because of the neglect of the Commissary, a department universally complained about, it was fully seven o'clock before rations could be obtained. Dinner therefore consisted of two cups of chocolate and dry bread, as money could buy neither meat nor drinkable wine. Having thus satisfied our appetites we retired early to our beds, which consisted of mattresses laid on the floor of the apartment. Our rest was disturbed by the mosquitoes which tormented us dreadfully.

Saturday 23rd
Our little party left Aldea Galleja on the following morning. For the first three miles the road passed through vineyards. The fruit was luxuriant, each plant having about six branches heavy with black grapes. The road was about ten yards wide and consisted of a fine, dry and deep soil in which our feet sank ankle deep with every step. The heat was so oppressive that before we had gone four miles I grew first drowsy and then cold before collapsing unconscious. My friend emptied the greater part of his water canteen over me before I felt strong enough to walk again. I then dragged myself on to a small village lying on top of a rising hill where I threw myself down on the steps of the church entrance and immediately fell asleep. McArthur watched me for the better part of an hour before I awoke much refreshed. A glass of lemonade at a nearby *Casa de Café* perfectly restored me. I had never encountered such heat – the sky was cloudless and there was not a breath of wind.

After a further mile we found some relief from the sun when we entered a grove of fir trees of luxuriant green. Small brushwood covered the soil. Here the road narrowed to a cart track but continued sandy and deep.

After a further two miles we overtook an unfortunate English woman with three small children and accompanied by a soldier-servant. She turned out to be the wife of a Sergeant-Major of the 48th Regiment, had been lost for nearly two days and was seeking to find somebody who could point her to the right road. Her provisions were exhausted and if we had not encountered her she might have starved. Our knapsacks and canteen, however, soon revived her spirits.

About an hour later we fell in with a detachment of carts carrying provisions and stores to the army. Here a bridge carried the road over a small deep river with swamps on either side. Breast works had been constructed to defend the pass but since an army could easily have by-passed it by marching to either side it was virtually useless. It was, though, undeniably an attractive spot: there were enormous fir trees, circular and sweeping to the ground like English park elms. Nearby were two houses where rice could be obtained and the area was so inviting we decided to rest and eat, particularly since there was no water available over the next 14 miles. Having had a good meal with a pint of weak and sour *vino de terra* we resumed our march. The first three miles continued through fir woods before the road opened onto a sparse landscape where, apart from some low cork woods, there were neither trees nor houses. After a further six or seven miles the road eventually climbed a low hill and from here we had distant views of Lisbon and the Tagus and to the south a long range of mountains and the fortified town of Palmela.

We journeyed on through the same bleak countryside. Our trek was briefly enlivened when wild deer passed within range of a fowling piece, but lacking a suitable weapon we consoled ourselves with the thought that venison was out of season. The distance to Pegoes was five leagues, yet although we had only rested for an hour it was not until ten that evening that some distant lights raised our drooping spirits. On reaching them they turned out to be the camp fires of a group of the 89th Regiment travelling to Lisbon from Talavera. Pegoes, where we were to end our journey for the day, lay a few hundred yards further on. Did a more miserable receptacle ever meet the weary pilgrim? It beggars all description. It consists of two houses inhabited and one half finished. My friend and self were obliged, fatigued as we were, to retire to the stable and in the manger lay down to refresh our exhausted limbs.

Sunday 24th
We rose at six next morning and, in an old pan found in a corner, contrived to boil a cake of chocolate which refreshed us more than our night's rest. Having breakfasted and packed Mula, we set off around eight for Vendas Novas. Officially this was rated at being three leagues distance away, or about twelve miles. But in Portugal distance is calculated in a straight line and when allowance is made for a winding route the Portuguese league is probably nearer six miles than four. At least the scenery was better than the previous day: there were plantations of firs, some of which the road passed through, and undulating countryside added variety. Yet the land is largely uncultivated and there were few signs of human habitation. After travelling about six miles we met the 83rd Regiment on its way to Lisbon while a further two miles on we encountered the miserable sight of the regiment's sick and wounded lying around a well a short distance from the road.

Nearby a few pines offered shelter from the parching heat of the sun, so we decided to take a brief rest and to refresh ourselves with a slice of cold boiled beef and a cup of wine. Near us stood a small black marble cross with an inscription denoting that a Lisboan merchant, Don Manual, had been murdered at this spot. The road continued over the heath. About two miles ahead it was shrouded in smoke, and, as we came nearer the heat became intense. A cork brushwood fire blazed around the road for a further two miles and we were soon enveloped in smoke. Mula was terrified and it was only with difficulty and after blindfolding her that we could persuade her to accompany us. At last, tremblingly, she did so. No Lord Mayor's cook after dressing a turtle dinner in July could have exhibited half such exhausted countenances as we did when we reached the village of Vendas Novas about one o'clock. We procured a decent billet and were able to immerse ourselves in water. Vendas Novas consisted of about 30 houses, all whitewashed, and also containing a large, ugly and unfinished sporting palace of the king's. We managed to purchase a good bottle of wine and after toasting mutual absent friends were both fast asleep by eight in the evening.

Monday 25th
We rose at six next morning having passed the night undisturbed by mosquitoes or any other vermin, and after breakfasting on a miserable

cup of chocolate, set off for Montemor Novo, four leagues away. Much of the country was uncultivated heath but broken up by small clumps of shrubs and firs. The brushwood, mainly of cork trees and heaths, grew to around six feet. The road undulated through hills and dales, occasionally opening out to give glimpses of distant views which at least alleviated some of the tedium of the march. After walking about six miles we took a narrow footpath, mistakenly thinking it might be a short cut. It took us into a deep valley where we came across two secluded cottages. Weary and thirsty we attempted to obtain a little wine and water. The door was slammed in our faces with unfeeling brutality. Our appeals to humanity went in vain and such sentiments appear unknown to them. It is thus that the millions of money and oceans of blood thrown away in the cause of this nation are almost universally returned. Seeing some brown earthenware lying on a bench at the door, and to avoid any punishment falling on our heads in the case of complaint, we encouraged Mula to trample it to pieces. We had more success at the second cottage, some 300 yards away. Gratitude was expressed for the sufferings the soldiers were enduring, and we were given wine and apples. In return we gave all the cold meat in our haversacks, no small gift.

The road ahead climbed a high hill, and from its top we had clear views of Montemor Castle, towering over the neighbouring territory. Gradually the road descended towards a small and beautifully situated coppice of cork trees. The scenery was spectacular. Tired from our journey and welcoming the shade, we decided to take an hour's break and, while my friend and the soldier rested, I sketched. The foreground was covered by large pieces of rock, and, beyond, through the recently barked cork trees, was a good view of the castle. My companions lay in the foreground. Two hundred yards beyond lay scattered pools of water, all that remained of the river by late summer. A three- arched bridge traversed the riverbed, and judging from the smooth gullies made in the banks the river must have swollen to a formidable stream when in full spate.

The road to Montemor climbed gently through woods of olive trees. The town looked close, scarcely half a mile away, but the road was circuitous and it took fully one-and-a-half hours to complete the journey. As the road neared the town it passed through vineyards, but the fruit was too close to the road for much to have survived the depredations of passing English detachments. The town we entered was called Montemor

Novo, distinguishing it from Montemor itself, the castle hill. Arriving about two o'clock we obtained a good billet upon an Excellency in the Rua Nova. Our host raised our spirits with an excellent cup of tea, a drink rarely found outside Lisbon. Since neither of the party felt ready for dinner, I took my portfolio and made the steep climb to the castle. It was about a mile in circumference and the ground rough and uneven. Once protected by high Moorish walls and a deep fosse, the keep and most of the outer wall were in ruins, but within was a convent, Da Inadatu, occupied by about twenty nuns of the Franciscan order. Several

Convent at Montemor. Henry Rooth after Henry Smith. *Journal in Spain and Portugal* (1909)

had light blue eyes, uncommon in Portugal, and were distinctly pretty. They were busy knitting by their windows – which were secured by strong iron cross bars. I must have been a welcome distraction and they chatted readily, asking many questions about the operations of the armies, but expressed much anxiety when told the British army had retreated. The ruined castle commanded impressive views of the surrounding countryside and before the development of heavy artillery guns it would, with its position and its good water supplies, have laughed a siege to scorn.

On my return to my billet I found our host very communicative, not least on the customs of the English. He related to us the sufferings of the town from the French on their march to Lisbon the previous year. After enjoying the best of food and the choicest of wines they would politely request the use of a wife or daughter for the night. Their host explained this modest demand dared not be refused. This simple circumstance is distressing evidence of the degraded state into which Portuguese society has fallen. Is there an Englishman, tho' sword pricked his breast, that would not rather have rushed upon it than have thus tamely surrendered his dearest rights? God forbid there should be.

Although we were provided with a good warm supper of soup and boiled fowl I was too weary to do it much justice. During the past two days my feet had been suffering badly from the journey and with every step my shoes filled with hot burning sand and gravel and this had destroyed the foot of my stocking. I now sported a painful blister nearly two inches long which I bathed in vinegar and used every means to harden it for the next day's journey.

Tuesday 26th
We rose next morning at around six, and, seeing none of the family stirring, left the house with the intention of having breakfast at the first coffee house we came across. None could be found, so we faced a sixteen-mile journey on an empty stomach. It was a sorry prospect but there was no alternative. The occasional solitary olive tree scattered across the heath seemed if anything to add to the misery of the scene. After about four miles we passed a detachment of wounded making their way to Lisbon. Having some chocolate in our haversacks we decided to turn off the road as soon as we came across a house within easy distance. Shortly we did so. Seeing a house about four fields from the road and with two or three people walking about, we went towards it. On arrival all doors and windows were barred against us. We knocked repeatedly only to be greeted with silence. Convinced the family were inside we resolved to make them pay for their lack of hospitality. After rummaging through outhouses for eggs we filled our haversacks with an old cock and a hen together with some fine branches of grapes. We then quietly retired to a nearby spring and had a breakfast of a slice of salt ration and wine.

The remainder of our day's march was over sandy heath with an occasional small plantation of olive trees. Arrailolos, our destination, was visible, but distance was deceptive. The castle seemed barely two miles away, but enquiry revealed it was nearer six. The vegetation was parched. Eventually the town, which had been hidden from sight by the Castle Hill, came into view. The town consisted on one long street with minor streets running off it. It lay between two hills, one dominated by the castle and the other by a large convent, a large square building now converted into a hospital.

After drinking a dish of chocolate McArthur and I walked up to the convent. We were confronted by the miserable spectacle of dying men in the last stages of existence. One poor soldier of the 58th Regiment lay in a distorted position, his eyes open and staring vacantly. I asked a comrade, who had lost both his legs and was lying nearby, whether his companion was in pain. To my surprise he replied '*I believe he is dead Sir for I have not seen him move for several minutes.*' He was right, he was dead, and I asked two soldiers to remove him. This was only one of many distressing sights all around us, yet those who were wounded but could walk seemed to take the situation very lightly. My friend and I then strolled towards the castle. By then it was night but there was sufficient moonlight to allow me to make a sketch of the surrounding countryside. It was nearly ten by the time we got to our beds.

I was suffering increasing trouble with my feet. Large blisters were forming under my toes and the skin had peeled off my left heel leaving a raw red place where it came into contact with the stocking. I again had applied vinegar trusting that it would harden up sufficiently by next morning to bear the heel of the shoe.

Wednesday 27th
At eight next morning I was woken by the Scotch pipes of a part of the Black Watch regiment in full march on its way to Lisbon. After swallowing a cup of chocolate the small party set off for Venda do Duque of which we had heard no very favourable accounts. My heel was too painful to bear the pressure of the shoe so I was compelled to march slipshod. The road to Venda do Duque, which was about three leagues away, passed across a plain. We crossed two dry river beds before reaching a small stream where we halted for some food. The old cock proved excellent eating. I pulled off my stockings and shoes, sitting, while we lunched, with my feet in the water. The heel of the stocking was bloody

from the gravel that had got into the wound and the pain while walking had been excruciating.

We arrived at Venda do Duque around midday. It was cheerless, consisting of little more than a single hovel-like house, but it was able to supply a good bottle of wine. Several glasses helped to raise my spirits, and having rested my feet I decided to concentrate my energies on one dash for Estremoz, three leagues away. A good billet could be found there and we could rest for a day. We started about two o'clock but had scarcely gone two miles before I began to repent of my temerity. Both feet sank under me with every step. At last arriving at a pool of water, I pulled off my footwear, washed and dried my feet and continued barefooted. My heel felt better for this but I worried that the blisters on my soles might burst. But about two miles from Estremoz a new road had recently been completed and surfaced with sharp gravel. This finished me. By the time we reached Estremoz both my feet left a bloody trail. Fortunately we were allocated a good billet and I retired immediately to bed.

Thursday 28th
From now on Peter McArthur and I were to go our separate ways, me moving on to Headquarters near Elvas, McArthur to join his regiment. Before leaving he drew on the Commissary for our rations and divided them up. We parted around midday, McArthur wishing me all good fortune. Feeling low in spirits I mounted Mula and occupied myself for two or three hours in sketching. The town was surrounded by fortifications and had four modern gates, but these would not have lasted against a regular army. The town was very neat and had several fine houses, particularly around the large open space where there was a fountain and water reservoir. I returned to my billet at around three, very much feeling the loss of my friend's company. I also missed the use of his servant who had expressed his attachment both to me and the mule which he had been looking after ever since I had acquired her. After cooking my rations and having some wine I discovered that there was a detachment of cars setting off that night towards Headquarters. Given the state of my feet this was a stroke of good fortune. Having confirmed this, and feeling lonely now McArthur had gone, I obtained permission to put my baggage in one of the cars, and, at ten that night mounted Mula and set off to Elvas, six leagues away.

LISBON AND THE ROAD TO ELVAS

Henry Smith's travels on the Peninsula 1809/10

27 July	Arrives Oporto
8 Aug	Sao João da Foz
21 Aug	Leaves for Lisbon
22 Aug	Lisbon
22 Sept	Aldea Galleja
23 Sept	Pegoes
24 Sept	Vendas Novas
25 Sept	Montemor
26 Sep	Arraiolos
26/7? Sep	Venda do Duque
27 Sep	Estremoz
28 Sep	Leaves Estremoz for Elvas
29 Sep	Elvas
30 Sep	Badajoz (Spain)
7 Oct	Talavera la Real
8 Oct	Montijo
11 Oct	Badajoz
17 Nov	Merida
15 Dec	Ann sets off from Lisbon. Leave of absence & leaves for Elvas
18 Dec	Meets Ann in Elvas
23 Dec	Leaves Elvas and arrives Estremoz
28 Dec	Arrives Lisbon

It proved to be a tedious and dusty march but at least I was able to rest my feet. I learned later that the baggage train was carrying money for the army, and this confirmed my strong suspicions aroused by the size of the guard, some 60 strong. The night was cold and a heavy dew fell. Day broke at about five. We passed a square old fort with its high central tower in ruins. This was one of the old forts ridiculed by Dumouriez in his history of Portugal, and, I concluded, with good reason, for on either side a heath stretched for several miles over any part of which a hostile army could have passed unmolested. At around seven o'clock the detachment reached a section of the road running between the vineyards that surrounded Elvas for two or three miles. The vine cutters were busy and willingly provided the passing troops with as much as they could eat.

Elvas, on approach, had all the hallmarks of a good frontier town, occupying the central hill of a group of three, each about 300 yards apart. All three were fortified, Elvas itself having high fortifications and deep fosses although dry at present. From a distance Elvas looked a fine town and had an impressive gateway, but once inside the walls the picture was very different. The streets were narrow and filthy with scarcely a single respectable-looking private house to be seen or any public buildings worthy of notice.

The aqueduct however was an elegant structure. Unlike the Lisbon aqueduct, formed of very high arches, that at Elvas was formed of rows of arches, one above the other with at places as many as six. Although it was only about a mile in length it was a hugely impressive structure.

Having committed Mula to the care of one of the car drivers I obtained a billet in an empty house in Rua da Sapateiro (Shoemakers' Lane) which, sadly, was a most filthy, dirty hole. Here I set to work cooking the remainder of my rations. None of the houses had grates in the kitchens so food had to be cooked over charcoal fires, usually in earthenware pots. Travelling through the Alentejo, one of the poorest parts of Portugal, the low standard of living was apparent. I have never yet seen more than a bit of bacon and two or three eggs for a whole family. But my bed was clean though, and that made up for the other shortcomings of the billet.

Chapter 5

Spain, Wellington and the British Army

Elvas to Badajoz

At six the next morning, Saturday 30th September, I set off from Elvas, with a palpitating heart, to travel to army headquarters in Spain. The journey to Badajoz took me three leagues across flat and parched countryside and it was while on the road that I had my first sight of the Commander-in-Chief, Sir Arthur Wellesley,[1] travelling with his staff towards Elvas. I pulled off my hat and was met with a long stare from the whole entourage.

Shortly after, having passed though a shallow stream, I crossed the frontier for the first time. My first encounter in Spain was with a flock of about 500 sheep, dirty, black-looking creatures, very small and protected by several large dogs. Viewed from below, Badajoz looked impressive. On the left, approaching from Elvas, rose the remains of an old fortification; the principal bastions of the town were on the water's edge. A long level bridge, with fortified gateways at either end, crossed the River Guadiana, and strong embankments had been thrown up to deepen and widen the river at the point where it passed under the walls. I journeyed through an encampment and a small park of artillery just outside the town and entered Badajoz at around ten o'clock. As was my custom on the march I made finding a billet the first priority, though this proved to be a long, frustrating and wearisome process. I found the billet officer, Captain Dawson Kelly, easily enough, but Kelly seemed very strict and demanded to know my name and regiment and said that his clear orders were to grant billets for one night only. I attempted to secure more and, for my pains, ended with nothing. Seeing him a gentleman I represented that I had come as a volunteer with strong recommendations to many of the staff but he again refused me a billet. Further appeals fell on deaf ears and, finding all entreaties in vain, I set off to find somewhere to stay until the next day when I intended to seek out General Charles Stewart and Colonel Waters and present my letters. It proved a miserable day, as bad as any I had experienced since leaving home in Bristol. I was worn out, tired beyond description, suffering acutely from my feet and compelled to traipse though the town to find a place to stay.

Poor Mula, laden with baggage, walked after me as we went from house to house attempting to explain my situation but all my efforts were in vain. I continued searching until five o'clock, nearly seven hours of tramping through the entire town and no doubt visiting many of the streets more than once. I thought of my friends in England, who, confident that I was now on the brink of success, would have been shocked to know the dire reality. Hotels or inns are unknown beyond Lisbon and neither I nor Mula, my companion in distress, had had a mouthful of food since the previous day. Each time I stopped at a door Mula wagged his tail, no doubt anticipating that our journey was about to end. Pulling the reluctant mule from one door to another I could not help patting him commiseratively on the neck. Our fates were inextricably linked, and I felt that Mula no doubt regarded me as a hard-hearted master. Eventually, passing a small hovel, Mula resisted, and, looking back, I saw him pitifully incline his head towards some water melons. His intentions were too clear to be misinterpreted, and I bought one, the size of a man's head, for three *reis*, about threepence. Retiring to a secluded spot we shared the melon between us. Mula seemed pleased, wagged his tail and followed me willingly for another hour.

About seven in the evening I spotted some soldiers buying cigars, and thinking a cigar might dispel the gloom that now overwhelmed me, I approached the shop and was comforted to find the landlady was an Irishwoman whose husband was with the main body of the army. She was doing a brisk trade. I explained my situation to her although with the white lie that I had been unable to find the billet master. She provided a decent mattress and a blanket for me – soldier's fare – and a small peat house for Mula. The mule, no sooner released from his load, began gleefully to roll himself around in all directions. My bed, though modest, was clean, and never in my life did I recollect feeling happier than when at last I stretched out on it at full length. Dusk was now setting in, and had I not tried my luck I would have been sleeping under the stars.

First setbacks: 'Interest is the god of all'

I was at Lt. Colonel Waters' lodging by nine o'clock to enquire when he would be available. I was told it would be around ten so I returned to

Sir John Waters (c.1836)
by William Salter
© National Portrait Gallery, London

'…even before he spoke my hopes plummeted'

my lodgings, drank some chocolate, and came back to the colonel's with the letters of introduction. I was shown up to a splendid apartment where two brilliant Light Horse officers were at breakfast. The colonel soon made his appearance, but even before he spoke my hopes plummeted. While hastily formed judgements are often wrong, I only wished that mine had proved so now. Waters was polite, pressed me to take a second breakfast, and then discussed the news of the day. I waited fruitlessly for nearly half an hour for an opportunity to speak to him on the reason for my visit. Eventually, when I asked directly when he might have ten minutes to spare, I was invited to dinner. When I returned at 3.30 the same officers were present. Finding it almost impossible to secure a word in private with Waters I had to explain my business to the group and show the letters I had brought, addressed to General Charles Stewart. I was placing high hopes on these but yet again I was thwarted by ill-luck: the general was confined to bed and far too ill to consider my letter. Frustrated, I felt compelled to explain my real situation in private to Waters. Although he expressed great sorrow at it he was at a loss as to how to advise me and stated bluntly that he himself had no interest in helping. Greatly hurt, I rose and politely wished the colonel a good evening.

I left the town as soon as I could by the nearest exit. I had plenty to think about as I took a solitary walk by the river, and all my reflections were sombre. I felt ashamed of my uniform and would have given anything for a plain coat and a round hat. All my hopes were dashed and I had no idea what to do or where to turn. My friends had been indefatigable in obtaining the letters I had brought with me but they carried no leverage: interest is the god of all. Every letter from which I could find the least prospect of securing a post had now been delivered apart from one to General Howe Campbell and he had returned to England. Yet I had got nowhere and a staff position looked a remoter prospect than ever. My best hopes now lay in obtaining an Ensigncy, but even that would take time and it might well lead to a posting to a West Indian regiment. In the meantime, while I waited for the King's appointment to arrive I could be attached to a regiment in Portugal as a private. That at least was what I had been told by several officers. The errors in my plan of action were now all too clear. What I *should* have done was to have procured an Ensigncy in England and then have brought letters of recommendation for a staff position. I might have been able to secure that in Portugal but not the Ensigncy as well. Lost in these melancholy reflections I had walked the better part of two miles before remembering that one of my mother's letters mentioned that my friend Dr Newman had written to Colonel Leighton of the 4th Dragoons hinting at the possibility of an introduction to Lord Edward Somerset. Somerset was at the time a constant companion of Wellington.

I then returned to the town in slightly better spirits and found on enquiry that the colonel was in Merida with an advanced detachment of the army. Mula not being fit enough to undertake the journey, I wrote as persuasive a letter as possible and enclosed that from Dr Newman. I then settled back to wait anxiously for three days for a reply. I was not permitted to draw rations during my time in Badajoz and so had to fend for myself. There were no butchers' stalls apart from the *contrador* to the Commissary and he was not allowed to sell to any English. My diet therefore consisted of chocolate and occasionally some bacon and a few eggs together with a hint of poor but expensive wine.

Henry Smith by William Hobday, c.1815. Courtesy Province of Bristol Freemasons

Charlotte Street, Queen Square: Henry Smith's birthplace by Henry Smith. Bristol Record Office, Richard Smith Papers

Madame Catalani in Semiramide by Robert Dighton.
© National Portrait Gallery, London
'Equally famous for her voice and her rapacity' (Latimer).

Henry 'Orator' Hunt by Adam Buck.
© National Portrait Gallery, London

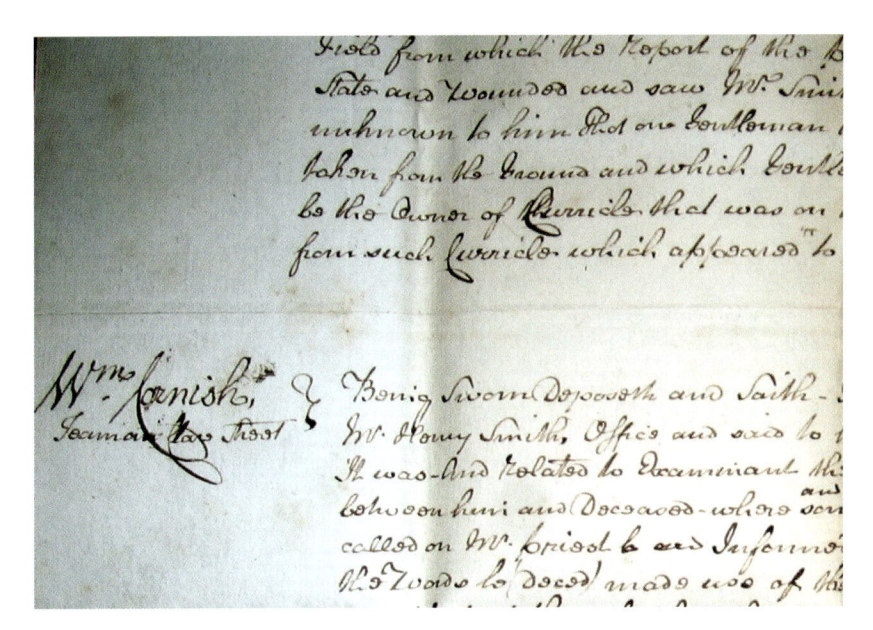

Testimony of William Cornish. Bristol Record Office.
'The jury no longer hesitated but returned a verdict of "wilful murder"…'

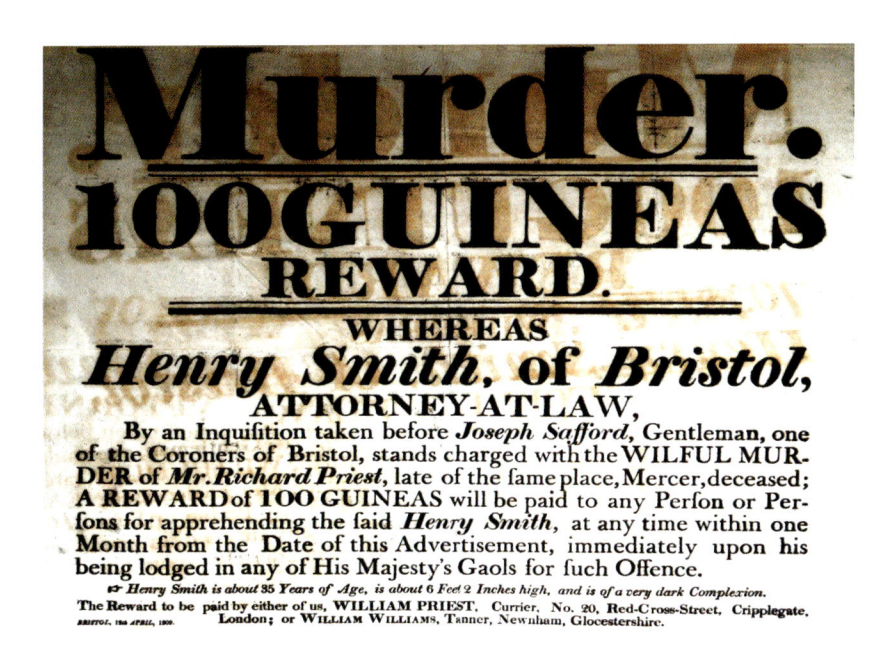

Murder.
100 GUINEAS REWARD.

WHEREAS
Henry Smith, of Bristol,
ATTORNEY-AT-LAW,
By an Inquisition taken before *Joseph Safford*, Gentleman, one of the Coroners of Bristol, stands charged with the **WILFUL MURDER** of *Mr. Richard Priest*, late of the same place, Mercer, deceased; A REWARD of 100 GUINEAS will be paid to any Person or Persons for apprehending the said *Henry Smith*, at any time within one Month from the Date of this Advertisement, immediately upon his being lodged in any of His Majesty's Gaols for such Offence.

☞ *Henry Smith is about 35 Years of Age, is about 6 Feet 2 Inches high, and is of a very dark Complexion.*
The Reward to be paid by either of us, WILLIAM PRIEST, Currier, No. 20, Red-Cross-Street, Cripplegate, London; or WILLIAM WILLIAMS, Tanner, Newnham, Glocestershire.

'100 guineas reward'. Courtesy Charles Wallis-Newport

Oporto, with Bridge of Boats 1809 by Henry Smith. Engraved by M Dubourg. © National Army Museum

Halt before Montemor, by Henry Rooth after Henry Smith. *Journal in Spain and Portugal* (1909)

The town Elvas, its Aqueduct and Fort Lucie 1809 by Henry Smith. Engraved by M Dubourg. © National Army Museum

Elvas, Forts La Lippe and Lucie. Troops on the march from Talavera 1809 by Henry Smith. Engraved by M Dubourg. © National Army Museum

Badajos on the Guadiana, as approached from Elvas by Henry Smith. Engraved by M Merke. © National Army Museum

Arthur Wellesley, 1st Duke of Wellington by Thomas Heaphy. © National Portrait Gallery, London

'He behaved … very politely [and] requested me to stay 'till his return from Lisbon.'

Ann Smith, née Creedy probably by William Hobday, c. 1815.
Courtesy Province of Bristol Freemasons

Richard Smith (1745-91), father of Henry. Artist unknown

The Butts near Tombs' Dock, 1825 by Thomas Rowbotham.
© Bristol's Museums, Galleries & Archives

Badajoz

Having little else to do I devoted most of the mornings to examining the fortifications of the town. It is completely surrounded by regular bastions with 20-foot-high parapets overlooking a wide, dry fosse. Each of the gates is fortified by drawbridges. I formed the view that Badajoz might be easily taken, and this would be especially easy once Fort Cristobal, on the opposite bank of the river, was in the hands of the besieging army.[2] At the top of the town was an old Moorish castle, parts of it still in ruins, and from here there are fine distant views, particularly towards Elvas.

The style of buildings is similar to Portugal but the town is much cleaner than those found there. There are only about ten shops, mostly concentrated in one street. There are several fruitiers and farriers and some cigar shops including that where I had gone on my first evening though the cutlery and linen factories are of English manufacture. How people secured a living is a mystery as very little appears to be happening and people seem to be largely self-sufficient. Hence the absence of butchers' shops: meat can only be bought on market day, held once a week. There are however a large number of priests having no connection with the convent but many of them married and living in private houses.

The exterior of the cathedral is not particularly noteworthy apart from its square tower, but the interior is handsome and the walls covered in crimson velvet. It was the only church I had seen on the Peninsula that had a regular choir similar to those found in England. The chanting is good but the solemnity of the organ was spoiled by the accompaniment of two violins and a clarinet. The altars in all the churches are very splendid, mostly covered with gilt and there is fine life-size statuary. High quality craftsmanship is evident, too, in the fine ceilings.

Spanish costume is varied. The women, whose figures are mostly well formed, know how to show them off to full advantage, and particularly around the leg and ankle. Bonnets are very rare and most wear veils, usually of black lace, or sometimes short cloaks reaching to the waist. Black is the prevailing colour at mass. The men wear large-brimmed hats and a wide girdle around the waist. Instead of coats they wear a heavy cloak thrown over one shoulder and use it as a wrap when needed. Badajoz is full of the military, mostly officers from Cuesta's army. Their uniforms are the reverse of the Portuguese with plenty of gold and silver decoration but displayed with very little taste. A sword crossing an olive branch is embroidered on the cape and many of the inhabitants, especially the clergy, have small images of Ferdinand VII on their hats. The uniforms of the patriots are poor, mostly blue or brown and with foraging caps. The officers appear to have considerable leeway in their choice of uniform, and those marching at the head of their companies bear little resemblance to their men. The dragoons are also a bright but varied lot wearing yellow or red uniforms and some have long *Toledos* and are all bold riders.

An unhappy Englishman

The letter to Col. Leighton had left Badajoz for Merida on 2nd October. The next few days, spent in every horror of suspense, were truly miserable. The kindness of my hostess provided some amelioration, and I was certain that she suspected not all was well. Her sympathy persuaded me to put up with many inconveniences rather than renew my search for better accommodation. Each morning and evening I stole to the Adjutant-General's office to enquire whether Col. Leighton had replied, and, each time, disappointed, quickly retraced my steps to the modest lodgings. The rest of the day I spent mainly in these spacious quarters, all of seven feet square and taking just two strides to cross and my mind was too ill at rest for reading or drawing.

I have heard that a companion in suffering lessens pain. I know not its truth but I did in some measure forget my own problems when I considered poor Mula whose piteous looks made clear that all was not well with him. I had made arrangements with a Light Dragoon to provide him with corn but the fellow must have been robbing either the King or his own horse: Mula had a good appetite and was emptying the basket within five minutes of it being filled.

At dusk, when the details of my regimentals were no longer visible, I used to wander through the town and on the ramparts to get some air. I was despondent and could scarcely believe a more mentally unhappy Englishman than me at that time broke bread in the Peninsula. Whichever way I turned the prospect appeared bleak. Ahead of me lay the hardships of a campaign in the position, at best, of a junior subaltern. A flinty pillow was part and parcel of a soldier's lot, and many a better man than I had endured them without a grumble. Soldiers become inured to hardship. My gloom deepened when I allowed my thoughts to wander to home where every suffering could be forgotten in the company of relations and friends. And there again my horizons were clouded because at the very moment which gave joy and laughter to the army, its re-embarkation for home, would for me alone bring an additional pang of misery as I must leave friends made through the hardships of a campaign and again launch myself into a sea of troubles. Home! When would the day come when I could once again be back in Bristol and quit of all care and danger?

First meeting with Wellington

Tuesday, Wednesday, Thursday and Friday have passed and yet there is still no word from Merida. I have no idea what steps to take or how to act. At one stage I resolved to go straight to the Commander-in-Chief, but the thought of doing so without an introductory letter and perhaps being refused admission until I had explained my situation to some puppy in an office denominated 'secretary' decided me to wait until tomorrow. Saturday the 7th and still no letter has come. With a sinking heart I left the Post Office and wandered through the ruins of the castle. My despair deepened, and, heartily sick of existence, I would have cheerfully headed a Forlorn Hope or undertaken anything, however desperate, that would have terminated things.[3] Misfortune seems to have targeted me as the particular object of her vengeance. Armed as I am with many letters to influential men I had built up hopes of getting a commission. But every one of my potential contacts was either away or too ill to help. My situation was becoming desperate. I had heard, however, that Wellington was expected at any moment to leave for Lisbon and it was not known when he would be back. I resolved to act promptly – it was better to know the worst than continue with false hopes. Having therefore decided to visit His Excellency without delay I was on my way home to equip myself appropriately when I chanced to meet an officer from Col. Leighton's regiment, the 4th Dragoons. He reported that two letters had been forwarded to Leighton who was at a small village beyond Merida at the extreme outpost of the army. But misfortune again dogged me: Leighton was very ill, so ill as to be incapable of duty. My letters all seemed doomed.

This latest setback confirmed me in my decision to seek out the Commander-in-Chief and so, at about 11 o'clock, with a bold external but a pounding heart I entered his headquarters. I waited on my own for some considerable time in an antechamber. Just as I was about to leave an inner door opened and two officers in plain blue greatcoats entered talking together, one carrying a bundle of papers. I politely asked the one with the papers if the General was available. He replied that he was, gave the papers to his companion and waited for me to speak. Thinking it was etiquette first to explain my business to the secretary I did so, stating my wish to serve in the army, handing over two letters of introduction and apologising for the circumstances that necessitated such a direct approach. Only then did I discover that I was talking to Wellington himself. The informality and total lack of pomp surrounding the Commander-in-Chief is astonishing. He read the letters from Colonels Baillie and Cole, said he knew them well and asked me my age, calling at the same time to General Sherbooke to find if there was any regulation governing the maximum age at which commissions could be given. Sherbooke replied that he thought not, merely that they could not be given to those under the age of sixteen. I clearly perceived that His Excellency disliked my original intention of joining the Portuguese army and perhaps saw my application to him as a second option. He behaved however very politely and requested me to stay in Badajoz until he had returned from Lisbon where he was going the next day.[4] He would then have considered my case. Bowing politely, I retired.

Journey to Montijo
Since I now had a week before Wellington could return, and my mule having now recovered from the journey, I decided to visit some old friends rather than remain in Badajoz. I had known some of the Buffs when in Oporto, and these were now stationed in Montijo. So, leaving my baggage with my hostess, I set off for the little town of Salamanca in the province of Estremadura, about three leagues away.[5] Between Badajoz and Salamanca the map showed the town of Puebla as well as several rivers but in fact there was not a vestige of it, as though some convulsion had destroyed it. The road crossed a level plain with a long range of hills to the right. The river Guadiana flowed nearby, extremely deep in some places, at others fordable by infantry or cavalry but intercepted in its course by islands and leaving many of its channels during the summer perfectly dry. Once I had passed the gardens and olive groves around Badajoz I had a clear view of Talavera la Real.[6] Arriving there about five

I resolved to try my luck in finding a billet and, after my experiences with Kelly in Badajoz, I was relieved to find an extremely helpful billeting officer. Captain Douglas Mercer of the 3rd Footguards went to great lengths to find me something despite the earlier arrival that day of three large detachments (every room capable of holding an officer having been occupied). At length a room was procured which could not be described as excellent but 'beggars cannot be choosers'. By the time I settled in it was dark and, feeling much fatigued and having fortified my insides before leaving Badajoz in case of short provisions on the journey, I soon retired to rest.

Next morning, Sunday 8th October, I arose with a violent cold. During the night the window casement had blown open, and glass only being found in the best houses, I had been in a cold draught. I spent an hour or so making a sketch from my bedroom window. Most of Talavera is built with mud walls, but there are a few decent buildings and one of the best in the sketch is the HQ of General Sherbrooke. I left for Montijo around eleven. It lay to the north of the Guadiana which I was instructed was best forded about four miles from the town. The road, which was wide, passed through olive woods at the end of which was a large encampment consisting of two Guards regiment, the 42nd, some German regiments and various others amounting to between five and six thousand troops. The scene was new and interesting. The encampment, ragged in appearance, bore all the hallmarks of men on active service. As I passed the men were cooking their dinners. The olive trees, which were providing firewood as well as building materials, had suffered badly, the boughs having been stuck in the earth to form the outer walls of huts and the roofs covered by intertwining rushes giving the appearance of a Hottentot hut. Water, drawn from the Guadiana, was plentiful.

I continued on slowly for another three miles, the road taking a winding route to the top of a hill, part of a range stretching to Merida. From the hilltop I had a good view of the plain below and of the River Guadiana snaking through it. About three miles beyond the river, encircled by olive woods, lay the towns of Puebla and Montijo. Evening was closing in rapidly on me and I was anxious to be on the other side of the river, but even with the aid of a spyglass no road was visible. Concluding I had been misinformed, or had overlooked a crossroads, I decided to take a direct route which took me over rough ground, populated by hundreds of fattening pigs. In the distance, again using my spyglass, I could make out a building which when I reached it turned out to be a mill. I paced the river for at least a mile each side of the mill without finding a ford. At last I recollected that a shallow was often to be found below a mill so I returned to the building and there found what appeared to be a possible crossing point. Rather than spend the night in the open I tried my luck in fording the river. I went cautiously for about forty yards, the water barely above the mule's hooves, and, half way across reckoned I had an easy passage. Ominously, though, the water began to deepen quickly, forcing me to raise my legs high to keep them dry. Then, in an instant, down we went. I was able to keep only my head above water. I struggled desperately to get my feet out of the stirrups. They were stuck fast. I made good use of my spurs and Mula responding with a series of springing motions, made it to the bank. Soaking, I quickly dismounted, and, to avoid a chill, completed the journey to Montijo on foot at a brisk trot.

When finally I arrived, sometime after seven, my friends gave me a hearty welcome and, seeing my sad plight, I was soon provided with a warm blanket. It had started to rain lightly before I reached Montijo, the first rainfall for months. By the next morning, Monday, it was torrential and a stream flowed through the town. If I had come a day earlier crossing the river, which had swollen several feet during the night, would have been impossible. The small towns of Montijo and Puebla are only a few hundred yards apart, virtually a single settlement. The surrounding countryside is devoted to corn, and the whole area for twenty miles around is one giant field of stubble. Puebla is one of the granaries of Spain, and much of the ground under it has been excavated to form great storage cellars. There are about five thousand British troops in cantonments, forming a respectable brigade, and looking in as good condition as though they were just commencing a campaign.

The heavy rain confined everybody to their houses. Although my friends had formed a joint mess, officers had been individually billeted. My companion had no books so I tried to use my time usefully by sketching the family on whom my friend was billeted while they had their dinner. The father would have made an excellent frontispiece for a modern version of the Knight of La Mancha and the rest of the family were in appearance an ill-natured group. The parlour was sparsely furnished and the bedroom a mere recess fronted by a curtain and with no other light. On the whitewashed walls hung a few miserable drawings of the crucifixion and various other religious scenes. The floors were made of a very soft red brick from which every footstep created dust, and the glassless window, well secured by iron bars, protruded from the house giving a view up and down the street. The Spaniards are abstemious, drinking little wine and making do with bacon and a few eggs for the family. Their main extravagance is tobacco which most men smoke from first thing in the morning until last thing at night.

A snake and indolent officers

The troops had an easy time of it with parades at nine in the morning and the full brigade assembling at five in the evening for half-an-hour. The remainder of the day, weather permitting, was spent in coursing, shooting and racing. There were plenty of hares, partridges and bustards, and, for those with rifles, kites and eagles provided target practice. There was also an abundance of lizards and snakes as I discovered when attacked by one of the latter. On Tuesday morning, beating in bushes for hares, I disturbed the creature, fully four feet in length and as thick as my wrist. I dismounted, and with whip in hand, pursued it on foot. My companions shouted at me to retreat but before I could respond the snake turned on me, raised its head and attacked. At that very moment I threw the whip at the snake which became entangled in the thongs and enabled me to make a retreat.

The indolence and idleness of an officer's life when not actively engaged in military operations was all too apparent. The whole corps possessed just one book, the rather odd choice of Smollett's *Roderick Random;* this had passed through the hands of every officer from colonel to ensign. On the first day after my arrival, when it poured with rain, I began to feel what verged on disgust at the military character. I visited several friends, some I found lounging in chairs, others asleep on their beds and others in that most elegant of attitudes: the elbows placed upon the windows and the hands supporting the head, the person watching the dirty stream running through the street carrying with it every species of filth. I soon grew tired of this, and although Badajoz held few attractions it was at least preferable to the life I was leading in Montijo.

On the road back I stopped to make a sketch of Badajoz and of Fort

Cristobal. The Guadiana runs between the fort and the city, but the fall of the fort would soon compel the surrender of the city. On returning to Badajoz I again called on the billeting officer, and, now able to report Wellington's instructions to me to wait in Badajoz, insisted on a billet. Major Kelly raised several objections until, after I peremptorily demanded a categorical yes or no, he finally gave me accommodation. This, which turned out to be in a priest's house with a good upstairs room at the front and a decent stable for Mula, was a great deal better than I had feared.

Should this journal ever find a reader they will no doubt feel disgust at the frequent references to this poor brute. But Mula is my companion and suffers the same deprivations as I do myself. Recently it is I who has been providing his feed and water, and, whenever I appear, he wags his tail. He knows my voice and would follow me like a dog. So my attachment is hardly to be wondered at and he is the only creature on the whole continent that unfailingly expresses pleasure in my company.

Although comfortably placed in my new billet its location created fresh difficulties. It was at the other end of town, away from the shops I knew, and, to add to complications, the dragoons having left the city with the Commander-in-Chief, new arrangements now had to be made for Mula's provisions which had to be carried home. Again, I would have given anything for a plain greatcoat for it seemed incongruous and even demeaning to be in uniform, epaulets on my shoulders, going into small, dirty shops to buy three or four onions and a cabbage and then, with six or eight pounds of corn for Mula in my haversack, to be stealing home with my own food wrapped in a handkerchief. I carefully avoided meeting the gaze of other officers in case my degraded situation would draw a contemptuous sneer. And that was only the start of it: I then had to start cooking, building my own charcoal fire before seating myself in the grubby chimney corner puffing and blowing away at the charcoal to keep the pot on the boil. The only consolation was the added zest it gave to my appetite. Food was astonishingly dear. An onion cost threepence or even eightpence for a large one, a small chicken cost 2/6d and wine was 1/6d a pint. Every type of food had risen nearly six-fold in price since Wellington had made Badajoz his headquarters.

The day after my return I went once more to the Adjutant General's office. Colonel Waters had instructed me to ask specifically for Mr

During, his particular friend, but, when I did so as before, he merely shook his head with the familiar answer *'no letter, Sir.'* I was stung to the root of my being with bitter disappointment. I turned from the room without a word and walked down the first residential street I came across. How could Colonel Leighton be so discourteous? Dr Newman's letter should have drawn a response, and at the very least mine should have received an answer. Perhaps there was some other explanation, and before forming a final judgement I decided to search the Post Office myself. The very first letter I saw was addressed to 'Henry Smith Esq'. Apparently it had been there for five or six days. So much for the friendship of Colonel Waters and his colleague.

After returning home I read Colonel Leighton's reply with great satisfaction. It was all I could have hoped for, promising he would use his utmost exertion with Lord Edward Somerset and written in an open straightforward manner. *'His utmost services would be mine with pleasure not only at the request of his old and valued friend Dr. N. but from a desire to be instrumental in seeing one of whom he had received so honourable and high a character.'* He asked to be told immediately what I wished. My spirits were raised: this small ray of friendship broke through the gloom of adversity which had hitherto darkened my prospects and poured the sunshine of comfort upon my dejected head – I felt comparatively as happy as before I had thought myself singularly wretched. I replied promptly, telling the colonel how my hopes had earlier been raised by Major Tidy's letters only to be disappointed by my inability to deliver them, and of the words of the Commander-in-Chief that it was in his power to give me a commission. If the best that I was likely to achieve was a subaltern's commission then I hoped that Colonel Leighton would be able to use his influence with Lord Somerset to have me attached to the 42nd Highlanders. My motives were twofold. First, there was a friend I greatly admired, John Henderson, who had a commission in the Black Watch. But secondly, I was looking to the future, for if the army was later to return to Britain I would be better disguised under the bonnet and vest of a Highlander's uniform.

The Belles of Badajoz

My mind now at rest, I was reconciled to accepting whatever came my way and making the best of it. I felt transformed, no longer oppressed by the anxieties that had made me unfit for society. I now walked confidently through the town, careless whom I might meet. One of the people I got to know well at this time was William Glascott, a lieutenant in the 16th Light Dragoons, who was billeted next door. The solitary lives we were both leading brought us together and ultimately we formed a joint mess together. Glascott was very clever but an eccentric obsessed with designing cottages. The walls of his billet and every scrap of paper he could lay his hands on were covered in drawings. We got to know each other well enough to visit without ceremony, and around 10.30 one morning I entered Glascott's room to find him wearing nothing but a shirt and so lost in concentration he was oblivious to my presence. Scratching out and redrawing he suddenly cursed and exclaimed '*Where could the kitchen be?*' In all other respects the plan was complete. I could not refrain from laughing and the startled Glascott turned. He explained that he had dreamed of the most perfect family cottage and as soon as he was awake he had attempted to get the design on paper. But the absent kitchen had spoiled it all and within moments he had reduced the design to fragments. Glascott was confined to Badajoz because of an injury to his legs suffered when his horse had fallen on him. I was later told by one of Glascott's fellow officers that he had been so lost in thought planning one of his buildings that he had allowed his half-blind charger to walk into a ditch.

Although my billet swarmed with vermin of every description, it was none the less an envied one. It faced the house of four beautiful senoritas, the toast of Badajoz, and my sleep was often disturbed by the midnight serenades of some enraptured suitor. The father kept a small tobacconist but gained status from his position as a lieutenant in the Patriot Army. The eldest girl was the prettiest, and I could pay her no greater compliment than describing her as the nearest in appearance to an English woman that I had yet encountered in Spain or Portugal; in my experience no woman on the continent could match the looks of their English counterparts. In the Peninsula a blooming cheek was rare and from youth to extreme old age women had sallow and cadaverous complexions. But not these girls, and every day I was greeted by my charming neighbours with gracious blown kisses.

There are several nunneries in Badajoz, very similar to those found elsewhere in the Peninsula with walls forty to fifty feet in height in which, some fifteen feet above ground level, are the small cross-barred and spiked windows of the nuns' cells. Each nunnery has a chapel attached in which is a large square or oblong grating, guarded by spikes, protecting the area in which the sisters gather to attend services. I went to a High Mass held prior to a sister taking her vows; the altar was richly decorated with twenty to thirty long candles, rosettes of artificial flowers and the convent's valuable collection of plate. The style of worship is very different to that in England. There are no seats so the congregation either kneeled or more commonly sat on the bare floor. The service, which was performed by the officiating priests at the altar and with their backs to the congregation, was in Latin although few understood it. At parts of the service members of the congregation responded by touching forehead, cheeks, nose and chin and often beating their left breast. At the initiation an anthem was well sung by three of the sisterhood accompanied by the organ.

Most nunneries have rooms set aside for friends and relatives to see and talk to the sisters. This is used most mornings by British officers although the younger nuns seldom appear. There seems to have been a shift in attitudes since the French had arrived in the Peninsula, and there are few of the younger generation who do not now prefer the bustle of the world to the sequestered and peaceful life of a nunnery. The sisterhood are very generous with their sweetmeats to the British who in turn purchase many of the articles made by the nuns. As in Portuguese nunneries there are two gratings, set about five feet apart, separating the sisters and their visitors, so the greatest liberty is the touching of fingertips. By the side of the gratings is a recess in the wall filled by a circular revolving cupboard so that the sweetmeats and purchased articles can be delivered to the visitors.

Waiting at the door of a great man

A few days later I had a friendly reply from Col. Leighton reporting that he had spoken to Lord Edward and handed him my letter. Meanwhile I settled down to wait for Wellington's return from Lisbon. When finally the Commander-in-Chief returned on the 29th all my hopes and fears were again raised. I waited for a further two days before summoning the resolve to return to face Headquarters. The ante-chamber was thronged with staff officers and in the midst of them was a small, dark, rather ugly woman but sporting a good figure. She was the centre of considerable attention, her conversation much courted and even my great lords did not pass her without lowering their topsails. I was later told she was the travelling convenience of His Excellency.

I paced the outer apartment for nearly an hour without exchanging a word with anyone and feeling distinctly uncomfortable. It is degrading thus for a gentleman to be compelled to wait at the door of a great man, where every tinselled puppy of a lackey who passes is sure to honour you with a sarcastic grin. At last a Major approached to ask my business. I mentioned Wellington's request that I should call on him after his return from Lisbon. After consulting the Commander-in-Chief the staff officer came back to report his message:

> *His lordship is particularly hurried, being just about to set off for Seville and he forgot to enquire of General Sir Charles Stewart, to whom your letter of recommendation was, but will write to him before he leaves Badajoz. Therefore will you please to call on him again on his return from Seville.*

While this message was being conveyed Wellington passed by without so much as a glance in my direction. I bowed and retired.

I was left yet again to reflect on my position and particularly the absence of an influential friend to speak for me: had there been one I would have been spared the additional weeks of solitude, misery and suspense that I was now doomed to wait. Moreover, all hopes of a good appointment were fading. This was confirmed by conversations with an officer in the 61st Foot Regiment who was in a position not unlike mine. I had been introduced by one of my old friends in the Buffs to Cornelius Alcock who was held in high regard by the regiment. Alcock, after suffering some family difficulties, had arrived in Portugal with an introductory letter to Sir Arthur Wellesley. He had then followed the army from Lisbon to Oporto, arriving there on the 9th May on the eve of the battle. After some uncertainty he was ordered to attach himself to the Buffs as a volunteer and in the meantime his name would be returned for a commission. He was ordered to assume the appearance of a private and to march with a musket and 30 rounds of ball cartridge. He was given privileges: excused guard duty, he was allowed to associate with the officers when off-duty and as a great favour these officers contrived to carry his baggage. He had fought at the Battle of Talavera and had only just received an Ensign's commission in the 61st. Ominously, Alcock had come across four or five people in the same situation. This story seemed to seal my fate. I feared I would feel highly indignant in this situation, but, having launched my bark at the guidance of my friends, I determined to refuse nothing. Yet having to dispose of Mula as well as a sword that had been presented to me by Major Golding and various other articles I should be disallowed from using, would cause some heartache. But if that was the best I could do, so be it.

While in Badajoz I got to know a mad-brained Irish Portuguese who held a post in one of the Commissariat departments. To my great relief, I had prevailed on him to grant me rations. Since arriving in Badajoz my money had been dwindling rapidly. The prices charged to the British were exorbitant, everything costing about three times its normal price. In the absence of locally produced butter people generally used Irish but this cost 3/6d a pound. Living as frugally as possible still took around a dollar and a half a day, sometimes two. Wine, which customarily cost about 6d per pint, was now priced at three times as much, and that applied to most produce. However, while obtaining rations was a great relief to my pocket, the procedure for collecting them took away much of the enjoyment. The abattoir was nearly a mile away and generally there was a wait of half an hour or so while the animal that was to provide my dinner was killed and butchered. Twenty or thirty head of cattle, placed in an open yard, were slaughtered at more or less the same time. Scales were not in use but a guess was made and roughly a pound of warm, quivering flesh was thrown to each waiting man by the military butcher. He was soaked in blood. Until I grew used to these scenes they had at first robbed me of much of my appetite. Since I had started to draw rations the only meat I ate was beef; bread, rationed at 1½ pounds per day, was not good and the wine still worse. Much of the morning was taken in drawing the rations and the evening in cooking and eating them. My breakfast generally consisted of chocolate since I was saving the tea I had brought from Lisbon until later; the rainy season was due soon, and after a long, wet and tiring day it would be particularly welcome.

I had become acquainted with Mr St. Pays, the brother of a contact in Lisbon. I had been given a courteous welcome and invitations to dinner where I dined with several senior officers. On one occasion I went so far as to seek St. Pay's influence with one of the Headquarters staff but, for my pains, received a long lecture from him on the impropriety of his interfering in military affairs: the opening sentence had told me it was a hopeless request.

My next attempt to secure an appointment also failed. Having heard that Lord Edward Somerset was in Badajoz, and happening to meet him near HQ, I introduced myself, briefly restated my situation and asked whether, following Col. Leighton's representations, Lord Somerset would use his influence with Wellington. He made no promise but merely bowed his head. He had previously told me that the Colonel had spoken to him in the highest terms about me but, judging from what happened on my next meeting with the C-in-C, this must have slipped his mind.

A few days later I had another letter from Col. Leighton asking after me and hoping that Lord Edward had been able to offer to use his influence. At least I had someone interested in my welfare although the pity was that he was so remote from HQ. Meanwhile, hearing that Col. Darroch had just arrived in Lisbon I wrote to him enclosing the letter from Major Tidy.

'The dreadful 15th November'

At length the dreadful 15th November came which blasted all my hopes and prospects. Wellington had returned from the south of Spain. I still held out some hope that he would be able to offer me a post, and determined this was the day to seek an answer. It started well enough. Having cleaned my best boots and pantaloons with the last drop of 'Day and Martin's Best Japan Blacking' which I had been saving for this occasion, and dressed myself in a clean shirt, I set off for HQ at about 10 o'clock. The same major who had spoken to me on my last visit detached himself from a group of officers and approached me sympathetically. I restated what I wanted and listed the letters I had brought. He spoke encouragingly, saying there was no doubt that Wellington would immediately grant me a commission. I stood around for half an hour or so until at last Wellington, his immediate business finished, came to the door and looked straight at me. I expected to be summoned into the inner apartment as his lordship beckoned to one of his staff. Within five minutes he reappeared, passed me with a polite bow and left the house without further word. The staff officer who had been summoned earlier then delivered a bleak and unadorned message: '*His Excellency has no opportunity of employing you at present, having numerous other applicants.*' I stood for a moment stupefied before, feeling tears welling up, quickly making a bow and a hasty exit.

So much for letters of introduction to great men. With the poet I exclaimed: '*Oh had I the wings of a dove, then would I flee away – distant should be my flight, there would I fix my dwelling, & in the desert escape the camp, where hypocrisy & deception reign triumphant.*'

It looked as though the Commander-in-Chief had now done his worst with me. Returning home, sunk in despondency, I was passing the house of St. Pays when he appeared and called me in. The wretchedness that must have been all too apparent on my face had drawn my host's sympathy, and for the first time I felt pleasure in his company. The only route now open to me was to offer myself as a volunteer. Even then it was necessary to petition Wellington to obtain his permission. This time St. Pays offered his services in delivering a message to his Excellency. It gave me another opportunity to explain my true position and I therefore returned home to prepare an address.

Chapter 6

The Black Watch, Ann and Return to Bristol

My petition

By 10 o'clock I had prepared my petition and left it with Mr St. Pays. It ran as follows:

To His Excellency Lord Wellington of Talavera & Baron Douro of the Douro[1]

May it please Yr Excellency Your Petitioner Henry Smith with most respectful apologies humbly addresses himself to your Excellency, praying you will please to take his situation into consideration. Your petitioner has served in England, but feeling desirous of seeing foreign service, proceeded under the strong recommendation of Major F S Tidy (late of your Excellency's Staff) to this peninsula with the intention of offering either his services to the British or Native Army bringing with him strong introductory letters to the persons enumerated below.

Yr Petitioner with the most sanguine hope that these letters would obtain him the honor of serving in the British Army, under the command of your Excellency, was induced at a considerable expense to equip himself with a mule and other necessaries for a campaign.

Yr. Petitioner having arrived at headquarters was singularly unfortunate: all the persons to whom his letters were directed being, either from illness or absence from thence on distant duty, prevented from rendering your petitioner that service with your Excellency in procuring him a commission which his strong introductory letters led him to hope for. Your Petitioner was therefore necessitated to introduce himself to your Excellency under the sanction of a letter from Colonel Cole (who served with your Excellency in India) when you were pleased to express yourself in language that did your petitioner honor – adding your desire to serve one who came so handsomely recommended requested your petitioner to repeat his call on your return from Lisbon.

Yr Petitioner now finding that no opportunity offers for employing him in that situation which his introductory letters as well as station in life gave him reason to hope & still feeling an ardent desire to serve under your Excellency he is induced to offer his services as a volunteer – & should it meet your Excellency's approbation your permitting him to serve in the second battalion of the 42nd will with most heartfelt gratitude be acknowledged by your Excellency's most obedient & very respectful petitioner Henry Smith.
<u>*16 November 1809 20 Campo l'Audo*</u>

Brigadier General Sir Charles Stewart; William Howe Campbell Colonels Stewart, 23rd Dragoons; Darroch, late Adjutant General; Leighton 4th Dragoons
Lieut. Col. John Walters & Campbell

Having left it I then settled down with patience, a feeling I had now become fully familiar with, to await Wellington's reply. But my face must have revealed my agitation and anxiety because, going to draw my rations, the 'mad commissary' saw that something was wrong and asked, with the greatest delicacy, if it was within his powers to help. If so, he was at my service. I admitted I had been ruffled. Stretching out his hand, he said:

'Let us be friends – I have met with too many crosses & misfortunes in life myself not to pity those who are suffering under their sting; you shall dine with me today and over a bottle of the best the store can afford we'll talk more of it. Solitude is not good for you.'

I readily accepted and agreed to return at four o'clock, reflecting how half of suffering is relieved by having a sympathetic ear: we cannot impart our sorrows to the senseless wall, the passing gale cannot be made the confidant of our cares. The commissary, Richard O'Hea, was worthy of filling a higher post than fortune had allotted him. He was from Ireland but had left there very young and since lived mainly in Lisbon. He was well acquainted with my sister-in-law's relatives, the Roberts, who lived there. After dinner he told his story, and the ups and downs of his life made my own sufferings seem lighter. He had left home at the age of eleven and joined the Royal Navy where he had served many years. He had not been in touch with any of his relatives for 14 years, all of whom he assumed thought him long dead. The only news of them he had heard was from an Irish officer he had met in Egypt who had told him that his father was dead and that his younger brother had inherited the estate. He wished him enjoyment of it for he had no intention of depriving him.

The Black Watch
At long last I received the orders for which I had been waiting. Wellington's instructions were precise: I was to report to Colonel the Lord Robert Blantrye of the 42nd Highlanders as a volunteer and to take the post of honour at the right of the Grenadiers.[2] The regiment was bivouacking in a cork wood near the ancient town of Merida, the advanced post of the British army. I departed for the town in good spirits for although I regarded the position as incommensurate with my station in life anything was better than continuing uncertainty. I made arrangement for my baggage, mounted Mula and bade adieu to Badajoz. The journey to Merida took two days and was uneventful. As so often, finding a place for the night was difficult, but with the help of a small bribe I persuaded a group of soldiers from the Royals to allow Mula in with their horses and I slept with the guard. It was as good a night's sleep as I had had since setting foot in the Peninsula.

Next morning I reported to the colonel who received me courteously but appeared astonished by Wellington's orders: '*Volunteer! Surely Sir to a gentleman a commission might be given.*'

I outlined my situation, explaining that a commission might defeat my chances of returning to England; this would depend on letters I was expecting. Blantyre bowed assent and introduced me to the adjutant with instructions to see me properly kitted out. The next day saw me metamorphosed into a Highlander. I flattered myself that the uniform became me although I was soon to experience its inconveniences. A sergeant of the Grenadiers instructed me in the use of the musket, and, having learnt to use it in the volunteers I was quickly passed fit for the line. The next task, the broadsword, was new to me and took some days to master, but within a week I fell into my post like an old soldier. When the corps was on duty I was armed with a musket and positioned on the right of the Grenadiers between a corporal and the Captain. John Campbell, the

Captain, is as fine a fellow as ever graced a kilt and his manliness of figure is equalled only by his urbanity of manner.

Little did I know at the time, however, that my service with the Black Watch was destined to be so brief. One day, as I was passing the commander's billet, a sergeant called to me and handed me a letter in that handwriting I knew so well. It was postmarked Lisbon. I hurried back to my quarters and, with pounding heart, read the letter. Could it be true? That my dear Ann was now in Portugal? That she had travelled alone from Bristol, braving who knows what dangers along the way, to seek out this poor unfortunate soul? She was, it transpired, now in Lisbon but would be leaving in three days, under the protection of a train of muleteers. She hoped to find me in Elvas. This turned affairs on their head. I explained the new situation at once to my friend John Campbell and he then accompanied me to Colonel Lord Blantyre, who handsomely gave me leave of absence for as long as my situation might require.

Arrival of Ann and journey to Lisbon

I hastened back to Badajoz and consulted with Richard O'Hea. Good friend that he was, he very kindly agreed to come with me to Elvas where the muleteers generally stopped. For three successive days we tramped the woods around Elvas and at night we returned to our billets dropping with fatigue. At last, on Monday the 18th December, we were able to make out a long train of muleteers in the distance. How can I relate my feelings when, after all my trials and sorrows, I was at last able to embrace again the one being in all the world dearest to me, and whom I feared I would never set eyes on again?

What a journey she had had, with the road from Lisbon to Elvas being no less perilous than the voyage. With only a muleteer as bodyguard she had courageously braved a journey across a country at war: the roads infested with bandits and deserters from the armies, and a beautiful golden-haired girl of nineteen attracted a great deal of attention, much of it unwanted. Dissolute monks posed a particular menace, one proving especially persistent. It took the threat of retribution from a British officer to force him to desist.

We stayed only a few days in Elvas before setting off for Lisbon on the 23rd December. Arriving in Estremoz about ten at night we had great difficulty in finding a place to stay. A grand convocation of monks was being held in the town and they had taken virtually every free bed. In our search for somewhere to spend the night we were accompanied by a British officer also in need of a bed. At last, around midnight, we found an inn of sorts. The family lay on the floors of the kitchen and parlour amidst their pigs. There was some conversation between our hostess and two rascals as ill-looking as any I had ever seen, and after about ten minutes I was beckoned to follow. Ann placed herself under my arm. Meanwhile my brother officer had quietly sunk onto the floor beside an old grunting sow and fallen sound asleep. I was about to follow our guides when a sudden thought of murder struck me. The appearance of our guides was enough to justify my suspicions. I immediately went over to my saddle that I had placed in one corner and took out my horse pistols from their holsters (which, knowing the road to be infested with bandits and marauding soldiers, I had loaded before we set off). I quickly put these under my coat on each side of my breast and then advanced. We were conducted up a long passage and through several rooms before at last coming to a great door. Following our guides we entered to find ourselves in a large and dusty apartment. My suspicions still alive, I kept our guides at a respectful distance in front of us. At the far end of the room was a small door. One of the guides, in a harsh and morose voice, exclaimed *Reste Signor*. We entered a narrow room, about 12 feet long but only four foot wide with a small lattice window, a fire hearth and a rudimentary bed in the far corner.

Our guides now left us to contemplate a spartan and uncomfortable prospect. We both feared for our safety. I consoled Ann as best as my own anxieties allowed. I feared murder but determined to be on the alert and, if it came to it, to sell our lives dearly. I took my pistols out to examine the priming. Ann asked if I had observed how one of our guides had eyed my figure and said his eyes had immediately fixed on the hilt of my pistols. I had not noticed this, but I thought it would be prudent to check whether our guides were lurking in the outside apartment and to barricade the door as well as possible. Taking one of the pistols I went warily into the apartment, treading very cautiously in case of trap doors. There was an air of faded grandeur about the place for, just perceptible through the dust and cobwebs, were the remnants of painted wainscots. As I continued into the room my attention was caught by something in the corner. At first I thought it was a man squatting on his haunches,

77, Largo S. Pedro de Alcantara, Lisbon
'We…obtained an excellent billet at the house of Donna Joanna Rosa de Pinto.'

but coming up close to it I found a richly embroidered saddle with some fine trappings. What, I said to myself, is this doing here? Its rich quality ill-matched the poverty of our guides and I conjectured that it might be the spoils of some murdered guest. I went on until I came to the door we had first entered. It was open. All was quiet. Conscious that the least noise would alert me to any approach I placed the saddle against the door and then returned to the bedroom. I placed myself on the side of the bed facing the door while Ann, totally exhausted, soon fell into a deep sleep. Eventually the morning light seeped into our wretched room. We had been undisturbed, although possibly we owed that to our hosts knowing we possessed firearms.

The next day we resumed our journey to Lisbon where we arrived on Thursday 28th December. There we were fortunate to obtain some excellent rooms at the house of Donna Joanna Rosa de Pinto at 77 Largo S. Pedro de Alcantara. It was superbly situated with splendid views across the city.

Return to Bristol

We remained there for some three weeks before, on Tuesday 22nd January 1810, Ann and I embarked on board the *Caesar*, an American brig, to sail back to England. The journey was mercifully uneventful and we arrived at Liverpool two weeks later on Monday 5th February. I had made up my mind: I had no realistic choice but to surrender and to face trial at the Assizes in the middle of April. I certainly had no wish to be incarcerated in Bristol gaol awaiting trial so I would have to lie low and to avoid anywhere I might be recognised. On the voyage we had become acquainted with a fellow passenger, Captain Ferguson, who has friends in Sutherland, and I accepted an invitation to spend time with him until nearer the date of the Assizes.

As Ann had now to return home we had to part, and on the day following our arrival she left Liverpool for Bristol. I had sent word to my Bristol friends almost the moment we arrived but delayed giving notice to the authorities until the 4th April when I wrote to Joseph Langley and Theodore Lawrence, Coroners of the City of Bristol, to say that I intended to surrender to the Sheriffs on 16th April in time for the Assizes. It was not until 8th April that I arrived in London to meet my old friend Dan Burges who was conducting my legal proceedings. There we held consultations with the distinguished counsellor, William Garrow. On Monday the 9th I set off for Salisbury and on the 11th took up quarters at Henry Hunt's house. The next day I moved to the house of another friend, William Clayfield, a scientist living in Castle Street, where I stayed until Monday 16th April, the day I had agreed to surrender. Then, early that morning, accompanied by James Lean, I went in my brother's carriage on the journey to Newgate.

Sir Henry Lippincott

The stench of Newgate was overpowering. I was not the only person surrendering that day for the Assizes. Sir Henry Lippincott, who was Colonel of the North Gloucester Militia Regiment, was also facing grave charges. He had been accused of felonious assault upon a woman whom, it was said, he had decoyed from the Cathedral. One Sunday last December he had been crossing College Green in the company of Captain Gregory, also of the North Gloucester Militia, when they had encountered two young women, Mary Milford and her friend Mary

Jones, outside the Cathedral. After a brief conversation the women had agreed to accompany the officers to a nearby house. Mary Jones had then gone with the Captain to his room, leaving her companion in the sitting room with Sir Henry. There, she claims, after offering her two guineas which she had refused, he had forced himself on her. She had resisted, struggling and shouting until, she says, she had fainted and Sir Henry had accomplished his purpose. Mary Jones was well known as a woman of the town, and why Sir Henry had had to avail himself of the services of such a strumpet had been much speculated upon by those who know him. I am told that Mary Milford had later applied through Sophia Jones, the sister of her friend, to Sir Henry for pecuniary recompense. He had refused this but, later, learning that charges were being brought against him, he had, like me, chosen to disappear.

My case

I then spent an anxious day and night. The previous year the coroner's verdict had arraigned me on a charge of murder. Tempers had been high and friends of Richard Priest were determined I should be held to account for his death. Many seemed to consider that I had acted high-handedly and that I could have settled the dispute without recourse to a duel. A year ago my friends, considering that I would face a malicious prosecution, had persuaded me to abscond.

  I could take some comfort that juries generally took a lenient view of duelling. Many duellists never had to face a court. This was true of an affair of honour that had taken place last September, when I was in the Peninsula, between George Canning, the Foreign Secretary, and the Minister of War, Lord Castlereagh. The scandal that ensued following their meeting on Putney Heath has forced both men to resign from office, yet there had been no trial because although Canning had, like Priest, been hit in the thigh, he had survived the injury. But when death occurs juries have sometimes convicted for murder, and there has recently been a notorious case concerning Major Campbell. This had taken place before my own unfortunate affair, but he had been found guilty of murder at his trial in Armagh some eighteen months or so back. The jury had recommended clemency and there had been a clamour for the major to be reprieved; the King however had refused to intercede and Campbell had been hanged.

I am unfortunate in the judge I have to face. The Recorder, Sir Vicary Gibbs, is Attorney General and famed for his acrid temper and lack of compassion, and thus sometimes known as Sir 'Vinegar' Gibbs. Nor can the reception he got when he arrived in Bristol have done anything for his temper. The government is unpopular for its repression and Sir Vicary had been prominent in this. For days before he arrived there had been handbills circulating saying '*No Gibbs*' and '*Burdett for ever; no Tower*. Gibbs was received into the City with groans and hisses from the populace, and, later, I was told, while he was being entertained by the Corporation at the Mansion House, just across from the house where I was born, a mob had smashed the windows. The crowd, who had been protesting against the imprisonment of Sir Francis Burdett in the Tower, had then gone on to demolish windows in the Council House and the Guildhall.

When the Court opened next day Sir Vicary had some warnings for those who had taken part in the disturbances. More worrying for me, however, was what he had to say about duelling and murder. He told the court

> *that if two men had a quarrel in the street, and proceeded in the height of passion to blows, and one of them shall be killed, it was considered as manslaughter – but if there was time for reflection, which in duels is generally the fact (the very arranging and fetching the weapons giving that time) the case is materially altered – and that if one falls, not only the person by whose hand he falls, but everyone aiding and abetting, either as second, or in any other capacity, is equally guilty of* murder.

It is a terrifying prospect. My lawyers have stressed that very point: in making my decision to surrender I must assume that it will be proved that Richard Priest had fallen by my hand and that the Recorder will tell the jury that homicide in a deliberate duel amounts to murder.

I had hoped that the lapse of time would have allowed the ill-feeling towards me in Bristol to have abated, but my friends had told me the minds of the middle and lower classes of society are still much inflamed. This had been fuelled a year ago by the declaration Priest had made to the surgeon's pupil when they had returned home from our meeting.

Sir Vicary Gibbs by Thomas Goff Lupton © National Portrait Gallery, London

'You will have ample cause for reflection for the remainder of your life.'

Placing his hand on his heart, Priest had reportedly said: '*I am a dying man. I hope God will forgive me and protect my wife and child. I did all I could to prevent it*'. This was manifest nonsense, but nothing he said could have been more prejudicial to me than that.

When Ann had made her dangerous journey to join me in Portugal she had carried arguments that if I returned and surrendered myself I stood every chance of being acquitted. The jury had to be persuaded that I had acted honourably and had had little choice but to accept the challenge. But, more tellingly, my lawyers had found irregularities in the way the Inquisition had been drawn up, irregularities that are so grave that it should prove impossible to convict me.

I have had assurances that the Grand Jury will be composed of men of the highest character and respectability who will recognise that the laws of honour would have rendered it impossible for me to have tamely submitted to such accusations from Priest. If I had refused the challenge I would have been stigmatised as a coward and shunned by former acquaintances. To be accused of lying is a violation of the point of honour between men, and only an ample and direct apology could have expiated it. Moreover, I bear His Majesty's Commission as a Lieutenant of the Grenadiers in the Bristol Volunteer Regiment. Sir Evan Baillie, M.P., Colonel of the Regiment, and a man greatly respected in the City, is prepared to appear on my behalf and to state to the court that if I had not resented the gross insult offered me I would have been dismissed the regiment in disgrace.

It is clear that such evidence will avail nothing in point of law but it may produce a material effect on the minds of the jury. My lawyers will emphasise that I come from a respectable family long established in Bristol and widely respected. Although my father died nearly twenty years ago many in the city still remember and esteem him as a fine surgeon, and my brother Richard, who succeeded him, has an extensive practice and is a surgeon at the Infirmary. My mother lives in the City, and is beloved by many.

It could have been that intervention from an experienced or influential party could have induced the deceased to apologise for his accusations of liar. But I do not wish to lay blame on my friends in this regard. Moreover, new information about Priest's circumstances have recently come to light which suggest that his future prospects lay under such a dark cloud that this may have influenced his behaviour. He had been deceiving his business partners. He had been given sole management of the business and its capital and had always appeared to maintain a profitable trade. But examination of the books since his death has revealed debts of upwards of £7,000. He had kept a false set of books which at the annual stocktaking gave all the appearances of a prosperous business. These facts must be handled with sensitivity, and while no one wants to speak ill of the dead these new revelations do suggest something of my opponent's character, and, living in perpetual fear of detection and disgrace, he may have been less anxious to preserve life than otherwise.

The trial

My trial was held on Thursday 19th April, and I was placed at the bar at 11 o'clock. The previous day Sir Henry Lippincott had come to the bar at the same time and he, after a severe trial, had been acquitted of charges of rape at six in the evening.

The Court was excessively crowded with many of my friends present. I was very ably represented by three counsel, Mr Henry Dampier, who knew Sir Vicary well, Mr John Smith and by Mr Ebenezer Ludlow. My counsel made much of my decision to return from service with the army in the Peninsula in order to stand trial, and they also emphasised the respectability of my family. The social disgrace and dishonour of shunning a challenge was made plain to the court. Yet the greater part of the trial proceedings were directed to the way in which the charges against me had been brought.

My lawyers contended that the inquisition had been drawn up by an ignorant man, that it has numerous defects and will not support a conviction. The inquisition was taken in the parish of Saint Stephen in the City and County of Bristol. It is on parchment, signed by the coroner but not by the jury, the signatures of the jury having been taken on paper. The pistol is said to have been *'then and there fired'*, applying to the parish of Saint Stephen in Bristol and not to the parish of Westbury in Gloucestershire where it was actually fired [in Kingsdown]. The parish of Westbury is not mentioned although it was there that our fatal meeting had taken place. The opinion of an eminent counsel, William Garrow, was taken only a week ago, and his view is that the inquisition is bad. My counsel laid out his arguments. It has long been the practice for the jurymen to sign the parchment to testify their concurrence in the verdict and the inquisition should have alleged that the pistol had been fired in some parish in Gloucestershire, not, as it implies, in Saint Stephen in Bristol. Moreover, the inquisition had failed to aver that the pistol was feloniously fired. An inquisition before a coroner for the death of another should be as formal and certain as any other indictment. In this case there were informalities in the document and it is clear that the coroner was a man wholly incapacitated to fulfil the duties of the office.

While the arguments were deployed I conducted myself with an outward show of firmness that I trust successfully belied my anxieties. After as long a three hours as I have ever experienced the verdict was reached and at 2 o'clock I was pronounced 'Not Guilty'. It was the informalities in the verdict of the coroner's inquisition that clinched the affair, and it was determined that the court could not enter into the matter. Mr Justice Gibbs warned that I *'will have ample cause of reflection'* for the remainder of my life. I shall not attempt to describe my feelings when I heard the verdict. My friends lost all decorum to the court, rushed towards me and I was literally carried by them out of court.

Postscript

Gordon House, Brighton, 1st March 1909

So ends the diary of my dear father. Such trials and tribulations he had been through, from the first unfortunate incident at the Theatre Royal to his final acquittal! My mother, too, had braved many dangers for his sake and my sister and I used often to hear the tale of their adventures from their lips. After being freed at the assizes, my father resumed his practice in Bristol, but it was not until two years later that, when my mother reached twenty-one years of age, they were finally able to marry, in the Queen Square Chapel, Bath, on 26th August 1812. My grandmother Augusta, a truly modest and pious woman, died at her home in College Street in 1814 universally respected. A son, named Richard John Henry after his father and grandfathers, was the first child born to my parents but he died when just a few days old. A second son followed in 1820 (my brother Richard Catcott Smith) then my sister Augusta and finally myself. My father was warmly welcomed back into Bristol society, resumed his practice and attained a captaincy in the North Gloucestershire Militia under Sir Henry Lippincott. He was also very active in his Lodge.

My father had already joined the ranks of Freemasonry before his flight to the Peninsula. As he later wrote 'At this period, whether occasioned by the Political feeling of Europe arising from the French Revolution, or from some other cause, this Lodge [the Lodge of Hospitality] ceased its Meetings until the year 1806...' when twelve members, including my father, '...renewed the labours of the craft at the Talbot Inn, Bath Street, Bristol.' The lodge later moved to Broad Quay, which they renamed 'Freemasons' Hall' and whose decoration he oversaw personally. In 1813 he became 'Worshipful Master' of the lodge and was involved in designing a new seal and arms when the title of 'Royal Sussex' was bestowed on it by the Duke of Sussex. He was appointed Deputy Provincial Grand Master a short time later and one of his most important duties in this office was directing the arrangements for the conversion of the new Masonic Hall at a cost of £2,000. One of the most notable features of the decorations were the paintings upon floor cloth which adorned the ceiling copied from Edward Bird, R.A. (a member of my father's

POSTSCRIPT

'This culminated in a terrible riot outside the Mansion House in Queen Square'

Detail from William Muller's *Queen Square on the Night of 30th October 1831*

lodge and well known to him). These included four pictures of the Cardinal Virtues, the model for one of which being my beloved mother. This picture may still be seen above the staircase at the Masons' new hall in Park Street. In 1822 he resigned his Masonic offices when he went into Wales but after his return to Bristol was again diligent in his duties until his final departure for the continent.

In 1822 my father was appointed as the Commissioner for Taking Oaths in the Court of Great Sessions of South Wales at the Maindee near Newport in Monmouthshire, and it was there that I was born on 13th October 1825. Our sojourn in Wales was, however, brief and we returned to Bristol in 1827, my father taking an agreeable house in Prince Street, not far from his birthplace in Queen Square. It was in this square that my father was to experience one more incident of drama in his native city, one whose consequences could have been most tragic for us all. In 1831 tensions over the Great Reform Bill then before Parliament were high throughout the land and not least in my native city. This culminated in a terrible riot outside the Mansion House in Queen Square where the Lord Mayor and other dignitaries were then dining. Houses were looted, buildings set on fire and all manner of violence was used by the mob. Many people brought furniture and treasures of all sorts to my father to keep, most of which were never reclaimed. He rendered great service

109

during the riots to Mr Humphreys, the governor of the gaol, whose life he saved by taking him from the gaol concealed under his cloak (the governor being but a little man and my father 6 foot two). Shortly after this incident, with a group of other public-spirited citizens, he became embroiled in the fighting when he tried to prevent looters entering houses in the square. He was stabbed twice but was fortunately nursed back to full and robust health. My sister and I (I being but six years of age at the time) watched terrified from the upstairs room of our house in Prince Street and afterwards my nurse took me to see the corpses of seven rioters who had been hanged.

Providence had never blessed my father with a great fortune and by the time I was ten years of age the costs of bringing up a family were becoming an increasing burden. The Continent, being a place where a man may more easily provide for his family in comfort, was settled on as our new home, and my father retired altogether from the law and left his native city for ever. Hence I spent most of my youth away from England. After some time in Bruges, when I was about 15 we moved to Malines, not far from Brussels, and took a house in the city centre in the market place called 'Bailles de Fer'. My father continued to paint and we still possess many of his charming watercolours of Bruges and other places. He was also, I believe, responsible for many of the illustrations in the series 'The Beauties of England and Wales', appealing to both his artistic and antiquarian interests.

In his last days my father was greatly troubled by the matter of my brother's involvement with Susanna Amelia Gardner, daughter of a rear admiral and the grand-niece of Lord Gardner. He married against my parents' wishes and after taking an oath that he was of age (which he was not). The marriage took place on 15th August 1840 and the news of this event may well have hastened my father's end, which took place the following morning at quarter past six (he died of apoplexy). What a shock his death was to us all, to our dear mother and to my sister and me, then still so young. The newspapers in Bristol reported (a similar notice appearing in the *Gentleman's Magazine*):

> Aug. 16 At Malines, Belgium, of apoplexy, aged 65 years, Mr. Henry Smith, late of this city. His remains were deposited in the Protestant Cemetery, his funeral having been attended to the grave by most of

POSTSCRIPT

the resident English, as a mark of respect to his memory.

The inscription on his grave read:

> Sacred
> to the memory of
> Henry Smith Esqr.
> of Bristol
> who died at Malines the 16th of Aug.
> 1840
> aged 64
> Regretted by a sorrowing family who
> in their grief have to lament
> in him an affectionate husband
> a tender father and a kind friend.

After our father's sudden demise my mother, brother, sister and I went to live in St. Oncer near Calais for a while, and from thence to Jersey but finally settled in Guernsey where we lived at a house called 'La Godaine' in George Road, St. Peter Port. It was here that we made the acquaintance of Mr and Mrs John Rooth and their three charming sons, John, James and Goodwin, that was to be of such import on our future lives. My brother Richard was at one time reading Medicine and thinking of returning to Bristol to take up practice there (where he would have been, as my uncle wrote, 'Richard the Third'). My brother was, however, sorry to say, nothing but a scapegrace, and he died on Guernsey in 1862 s.p. and was buried near our beloved mother (who was lost to us in 1857) in the churchyard in St Peter Port. The last of the Smiths.

After our mother's decease my sister and I went to live in London, where the Rooths had moved a short time before. Augusta married Goodwin at St Pancras New Church in 1858, and four children were later born to them. My own marriage to John Rooth followed four years later and three sons, John, Richard Alexander and James followed. How much I regret that my beloved parents never lived to see any of their grandchildren. The four boys have certainly not disgraced the family name: my eldest son John has, like his father and grandfather, entered the law and a few years since was appointed a judge of the Supreme

Court of Western Australia in Perth. Alex is a major in the Royal Dublin Fusiliers and when the regiment was posted to India some years back I joined him and his wife on a long and interesting visit to that country. I am also blessed in my old age by the presence of my two little grandchildren, Richard and Nancy. James is, like his great-grandfather, Richard, a fine surgeon in Brighton, where I now reside. My sister Augusta sadly died three years ago leaving a son and two daughters. Beatrice has made a good marriage to Mr Hayward and has a young son, Jack, though Mabel remains unmarried. Her son Harry (who has distinguished himself at the bar) is about to set off with his wife Beatrice on a trip to the Peninsula, where he will be following the journey made by his grandfather and namesake a century ago, leaving their little son John with us in Brighton.

My father's diary sits beside me now on the table as I write and it will be, I hope, treasured by my children and grandchildren in future years, as a lasting memorial of the life and adventures of their illustrious forbear.

Elizabeth Creedy Rooth

Chapter 7

Henry Smith: his family, friends and profession

The City of Bristol

By the time of the duel in 1809 Bristol's golden age had come to an end. For much of the previous century the city had prospered and expanded, rapidly drawing ahead of its English provincial rivals such as Norwich and York to become second only to London in size and wealth. Much of this prosperity was based on international trade. In Bristol, a contemporary observer commented, 'the very clergy talk of nothing but trade and how to turn a penny, all are in a hurry, running up and down with cloudy looks and busy faces, loading, carrying and unloading goods and merchandizes of all sorts from place to place; for the trade of many nations is drawn hither by the industry and opulency of the people.'[1] Trade with Ireland was the mainstay, but Bristol was superbly situated to benefit from the most dynamic areas of the eighteenth-century international economy: a more exotic trade with Africa, the West Indies and the North American colonies had grown spectacularly, a trade defiled by the traffic in slaves, but one that had brought Bristol great prosperity. Imports of tobacco, timber, cotton, rum and, above all, sugar, flooded into Bristol's warehouses.[2] Many of these products provided a basis for thriving processing industries: by the middle of the century, for example, the city had sixteen sugar refineries and numerous distilleries.

The city's population grew fast. In 1700 it had been around 20,000 and by 1750 it had reached approximately 50,000, well ahead of Norwich and second only to London.[3] Bristolians were noted for their independent spirit and pride in their city and themselves; in the late eighteenth century, 'Marmaduke Rawdon of York noted that Bristol freemen were as proud as Roman senators, and sparing with their hats, that is they were reluctant to doff them to their "superiors".'[4]

By the time of Henry's birth in 1774, however, Bristol was facing powerful challenges from the newer industrial towns, and notably from the fast-growing ports of Glasgow and Liverpool. Its population

Cathedral and College Green from Great George Street, 1827 by Thomas Rowbotham. © Bristol's Museums, Galleries & Archives

continued to grow, but more slowly, reaching 68,000 by 1801. Well before the end of the century Bristol had surrendered its position as the second city in England, and by 1800 not only was it only the sixth largest British city but it had fallen to eighth place among British outports.[5] Competition from Liverpool, the American War of Independence, the disruption of maritime commerce through war with France from 1793 and the abolition of the slave trade in 1807 contributed to the city's failure to keep pace with the newer manufacturing centres of the North and Midlands. The cotton industry failed to develop in the city; sugar, brass and glass production went into decline. Abraham Darby left Bristol for Coalbrookdale when his advanced ideas for iron production received no backing from local investors. Buchanan and Cossons cite 'a certain complacency and inertia [from the prominent mercantile families] which was a serious handicap in the adjustment to new conditions in the Industrial Revolution period.'[6] It is an interpretation that the nineteenth-century historian of Bristol, John Latimer, would have agreed with but probably have found too mild. He himself was scathing in his castigation of the city's leadership: 'As is not infrequently the case in ancient and solidly founded communities, Bristol was too wealthy to be enterprising, and many of her influential sons, having become rich in the beaten paths of commerce, were opposed through selfishness or indolence to the striking out of new ones.'[7] The city's elite was slow to recognise the advantages of better port facilities. By the middle of the century Bristol's position on the Avon was no longer the advantage it had once been. The narrow gorge and tortuous course of the tidal river had become an increasing handicap, the more so as ships became larger, and although attempts to deal with this were made in the eighteenth century they were too modest and could not match the wet dock of Liverpool which had been opened in 1724.[8] More ambitious plans were implemented between 1804 and 1809 when the Bristol Dock Company constructed a floating harbour and the New Cut, but the advantages of these improvements were largely negated by prohibitive harbour dues and by changes in the patterns of trade. All this undoubtedly contributed to the relative decline of Bristol but, as Walter Minchinton concluded, the fundamental factor at work was the shift in the economic centre of gravity of Great Britain.[9]

The physical fabric of the city had changed dramatically over the course of the century. As wealth and population had increased in the eighteenth century, Bristol business confidence was reflected in a series of new building schemes. An early and fine example of this was Queen Square, the construction of which had begun in 1699. Lobel and Carus-Wilson commented that '[w]ith the exception of Lincoln's Inn Fields in London the square was the largest in the kingdom and a fitting testimony to the public pride and taste of the city's *élite* and to the skill of the building crafts and architects.'[10] The increasing tendency of the middle class in eighteenth-century Bristol to move out of 'the cramped and noisy city centre to purpose-built squares and suburbs'[11] is well reflected in the houses of Henry's father, Richard Smith, who on his marriage in 1771 moved out of his father's brewery in Counterslip and went to Queen Square, and, much later, to the newly fashionable suburb of Clifton where 'purer air' was to be found.

Family: grandparents and father

At the beginning of 1809 Henry Smith had recently turned 34, was unmarried and living with his mother near Bristol Cathedral in College Street. He had trained as an attorney, had been in practice for about ten years and had an office in St. Stephen's Avenue. His family was well-rooted in the life of the city. Henry was himself a keen amateur genealogist and loved drawing up illustrated family trees, a number of which survive. At the top of the most elaborate of his efforts is the impressive figure of one 'Richard Smith, Sheriff of Bristol 1568, Mayor 1606, the founder of the Smiths'. He is presumably that Richard Smith 'Alderman of Bristol' who died in 1609.[12] However, although described on the tree as Henry's great-great grandfather, there is no evidence to support the claim of any early connections of the Smith family to Bristol, and this seems to have been the product of wishful thinking on Henry's part.

Instead, the earliest Smith of whom there is clear evidence was **Walter Smith**, a currier of Westbury (c.1640-1693). He was the father of **Richard Smith**, a maltster in the Wiltshire town of Warminster (which supplied the Bristol breweries with much of their malt). His son Richard (Henry's grandfather) settled in Bristol about 1741, when he married Elizabeth, the daughter of a Bristol brewer, William Bradford, whose business was based in the Counterslip in the parish of Temple. Richard had a brewery in nearby Temple Street but was also in partnership with his father-in-law. From his grandson Richard's account of him he was far from the image of a thrusting eighteenth-century businessman: 'Elegant in his manners and person, delighting in books, and hating the bustle of the world, he spent whole days in his study, leaving to his active and intelligent wife the care of his ledger and the general management of his business. No two people could be much more unlike each other. He was sedate, slow of speech, mild and placid in his disposition, disposed to take the world as it went while she was quick and irritable, knew how to scold when she thought there was occasion, which was somewhat frequently the case....The joke of the parish was that 'Smith and his wife seemed to agree on only one point and that was the getting of children.'[13]

Richard the Surgeon, their eldest son and father of Henry, was born in 1745. Some of his colourful early life is set out by his son in his *Memoirs* preserved at the Bristol Record Office. From this emerges the picture of a strongly independent and restless individual, very capable when focused on the task in hand but with a taste for extravagance apparent from early in his life. He was educated at Winchester College where 'his schoolwork was exceedingly idle and neglected, [he was] very seldom prepared with his lesson, and that he was in consequence pretty regularly flogged [though] the birch made [little]... impression upon him. He used to laugh at it and... seemed to be but little susceptible of bodily harm... He had also a bold ... temper which made him always ready to lead on the boys when in battle with the townspeople or in a predatory expedition against an orchard or a farmyard. It does not appear, however, that he had any lack of intellect or talent when he had an object in view... when he was at Winchester there was a grand visitation by the Chancellor and several noblemen and Mr Smith was asked to chant the .. *benedicte nobis domine* before ... dinner. In this he excelled himself so well that he not only was introduced to the guests but had a guinea slipped into his hand by Lord Berkeley.'

Richard appeared to have no desire to follow his father and grandfather into the brewing trade, leaving the continuation of the business to his sisters, and decided upon medicine. On leaving Winchester he was immediately apprenticed to a Mr Townsend, surgeon of Bristol, as the custom then was in the medical profession, for which his father paid £200.[14] John Townsend practised in Broad Street and had then been surgeon to the Infirmary for twelve years. While in time Dick proved to be a fine surgeon, things did not initially go smoothly for him. Townsend was a severe disciplinarian, and Smith a spirited young man with a rebellious streak. 'He disliked the profession so much .... that he sometimes refused to go there when at home and was persuaded to return with the greatest difficulty.' In the third year of his apprenticeship matters came to a head. One night Mr S. came home just at the hour of 11. Townsend had just locked the door and told Smith 'with a growl' to go about his business. '*Sir,*' said the apprentice, '*The quarter boys are now going and Christchurch has not yet finished striking.*' '*I don't care anything about it.*' said Mr Townsend, '*My clock has struck and that's enough for me.*' On saying which, he went off to bed leaving Dick outside in the street. However, 'The apprentice had the presence of mind to call the watch and to have him take notice he was at the door before the parish clock had done. The next morning an altercation took place, the master would

6, Charlotte Street, Queen Square, Henry Smith's birthplace

neither allow the apprentice to come into his house, nor return any part of the fee. An action was brought in which Mr Smith was allowed to tell his own case and plead for himself and the result was a verdict with sentence as to the quantity of money to be returned. The parties were, however, very good friends afterwards and ....Mr Townsend, although a surly man, was not of an unforgiving disposition.'

After this, about 1765, as was often the practice, he commenced his medical studies in London. There is a story that he was stopped by a Dr Colin Mackenzie when going to deliver a child dressed in a cloak and holding a sword 'as was then the mode'. The doctor reminded him of the '*impropriety of a man's going armed to bring a being into the world when such a weapon could only serve to send a man out of it,*' and asked him to remove it at once. Smith's answer is not recorded. Even in his youth he seems to have spent freely and clearly he was something of a dandy. Visiting relations in Warminster he 'made a most dashing appearance, being exceedingly handsome and dressed out in a blue velvet coat, pink satin waistcoat, [and] milk white silk stockings with gold clocks.' His father appeared to be tiring of the expense of Dick's education and his extravagance. Having given him fifty guineas, which had clearly not lasted as long as intended, he asked him, '*Dick, what have you done with the money I gave to you?*' His son replied, '*Spent it, Sir, and I thank God I am as happy when 'tis gone as when I have it.*'

In 1768 he was elected Surgeon to St. Peter's Hospital, Bristol, and supplemented this with a busy private practice in a room at his father's brewery in Temple. His eldest sister Elizabeth records that 'patients poured in upon him so fast that his father gave him a sort of cock loft in the brewery which he fitted as a surgery and... there used to mount men and women, gentle and simple, such a cataband [sic] ... that there was no end to them and we were all heartily glad when he went to Queen Square.'

It was at the beginning of 1771 that he made this move, leaving Counterslip and going to 'the last house in Charlotte Street at the corner of Queen Square opposite the gable end of the Mansion House'. This house, as far is as known alone of all the houses of the Smiths in Bristol, is still standing, a handsome though not grand Queen Anne building of c.1705. His move there was in anticipation of his marriage: on the 23rd September he married Augusta Catcott.

Augusta's family: the Catcotts

Augusta was the daughter of the **Rev. Alexander Stopford Catcott** who had been a prominent figure in the life of Bristol in the first half of the century. He was a noted classical scholar and poet, but his main contribution to Bristol life was as a headmaster, clergyman and theologian. He had been a Fellow of St. John's College Oxford before being elected headmaster of Bristol Grammar School in 1722. He then resigned his fellowship and the family moved to Bristol where they lived in the school.[15] 'He was an outstanding principal, appreciably raising school numbers and including among his pupils Dr Thomas Fry, later President of St John's College Oxford and Richard Woodward, later Bishop of Cloyne.'[16] Catcott kept this position until 1743, when he became rector of St Stephen's, Bristol, retaining this until his death in 1749. He was a prominent member of Bristol society and served as reader in the Lord Mayor's Chapel from 1729. After his move to Bristol he largely abandoned poetry and focused increasingly on theology (he was a fine preacher), especially his dedication to the Hutchinsonian cause, and published a number of books, including *The Superior and Inferior Elohim* of 1736.

Alexander Catcott and his wife Martha (née Symes) brought no fewer than fifteen children into the world, but only five lived to adulthood. Augusta, who had been born in 1738, was the only one who married and left any children. Her brothers **Alexander** and **George Symes Catcott** were also heavily involved in the life of the city.[17] Alexander Catcott the Younger followed his father into the priesthood, becoming vicar of Temple Church in 1766. He also took up his father's cause as an advocate of Hutchinsonianism, published several books, notably *A Treatise on the Deluge*, and was a well respected geologist.[18] His brother George Symes Catcott (1729-1802) was cut from rather different cloth, a great eccentric and (in)famous Bristol character.[19] He was a pewterer, in partnership with Henry Burgum, but is best known as a patron of Thomas Chatterton, the controversial and brilliant young poet and satirist who died at the age of seventeen.[20] Much of the controversy surrounding Chatterton centered on the poems of Rowley, 'discovered' in the muniment rooms of St. Mary Redcliffe Church: George, convinced of the authenticity of the 'discoveries', was instrumental in bringing Chatterton's work to public attention, and was the initial publisher of the *Rowley* manuscripts.

The Prime and Death of Richard Smith

In December 1774 Dr Ludlow resigned as Surgeon to the Infirmary and Richard was elected, just thirteen days before his son Henry was born. Smith remained at the Infirmary for the rest of his life and his portrait still gazes out from the boardroom. He was elected as Senior Surgeon in 1791. He is described as 'tall, handsome, of a slight but athletic figure, with bright eyes and beautifully white teeth'.[21] He was kind hearted, generous but impetuous and ready to fight when occasion arose. The Infirmary was staffed by some hot-tempered, colourful characters and Smith was not averse to physical fights with his colleagues if provoked. He even challenged a fellow surgeon, Dr Rigge, to a duel on Brandon Hill. Although the two men met the following morning, together with their seconds, pistols at the ready, Rigge at the last moment although 'by nature inflexible and courageous, but being undoubtedly the aggressor in this business…at last consented to make an apology' and no shots were fired. [22]

In the early days of his marriage it appears that he lived modestly, but 'In 1784 he became acquainted with the family of John Archer Esquire of Welford in the County of Berks, a circumstance which had great influence upon all the subsequent actions of his life; the first affect was an alteration in his residence.' Indeed in 1785 the family left Queen Square and moved to the Lower Green (perhaps number 7, where his sister Elizabeth later lived), to 'the late Mr Delprat's house, opposite St. Augustine's church.' It may be that this new house was larger and more suited to the lavish entertaining which Richard now began to indulge in. Archer was a man of great wealth who lived in a convivial, extravagant style and had taken such a liking to Smith that he came to live in Bristol to be near him; this did Smith's finances no good. By a combination of his infirmary work and private practice, aided by his growing reputation within the city, he was earning some £1800 a year by 1790.[23] He spent, however, even more liberally than he earned, much to the distress of his modest and pious wife Augusta.

Evidently, apart from Richard Smith's extravagancies, all was going well for the family. By 1790 Richard

> had now been at the infirmary nearly seventeen years and appeared at the very zenith of health and prosperity. It depended only upon himself to make a handsome provision for his family; his two sons were apprenticed to him and there was every prospect that his declining old age would thereafter have thrown into their hands a lucrative and highly respectable business, for it had entered into the contemplation of no-one that a frame so robust would have been so speedily overthrown.

Tragically, however, having been taken ill suddenly after an arduous ride during the hot summer of 1791, he fell into a rapid decline and died on 21st June aged just 45.

> Regret was painted on the countenance of almost everyone in the street and Bristol seemed to have experienced some public calamity. His remains were carried amidst the tears of a great multitude of

persons to Temple Church where they were deposited in the family vault, but afterwards removed to the upper end of the burials' ground.

The new professionals: surgeons and attorneys

Richard Smith's untimely death meant difficult decisions had to be made, not least over the professional training of his two sons. Richard was 'turned over' to another surgeon, while Henry gave up on medicine altogether and became indentured to Mr Robert Payne, an attorney. Augusta and the boys moved to 17, College Street (on which the Council House now stands) where Augusta remained until her death in 1814.

Richard 'the fourth' (1772-1843) was to become a well-known surgeon and one of the most prominent citizens of Bristol in his day. Henry's older brother, he had been born at Queen Square on 28th June 1772. He attended first Bristol Grammar School, like his father before him, and afterwards was sent to Reading School, then under the long and distinguished headmastership of Dr Richard Valpy. He was elected surgeon to the Infirmary in 1796 and succeeded to his father's old position of Senior Surgeon in 1811. He was instrumental in setting up systematic anatomy lectures in Bristol and was regarded in some quarters as the most eminent surgeon in England outside London.[24]

Successful surgeons could earn a very good living, and by the time Henry's father entered the profession the status of surgeons was on the rise. Originally considered inferior to the more 'gentlemanly' physicians, of whom there were only three or four in practice in Bristol in the 1720s, the title of surgeon or 'barber-surgeon' (even by 1700 there were approximately ninety practitioners in Bristol) in fact covered a wide range of persons of often radically different social standing. At one end were men such as James Parsley, the 'last remnant of barber-surgery' (died 1807) who 'dressed wigs, shaved, let blood and drew teeth'[25] to surgeons with highly lucrative, prestigious practices. By 1800 the professional scene of a century earlier had been transformed: 'the surgeons had dissociated themselves from the barbers, and the "pure" or hospital surgeon had become a specialist of high reputation'.[26] They were complemented by apothecaries, who made up and dispensed medicine.

In contrast to the university-trained physicians, both surgeons and apothecaries were trained by apprenticeship, which throughout most of the eighteenth century 'was an institution that continued to structure all

Richard Smith junior (1772-1843), surgeon to the Bristol Royal Infirmary 1796-1843, by John Hazlitt, 1824.
Wellcome Library, London

medical and surgical practice... the apprentice made up the medicines or surgical dressings, kept the shop tidy [and] visited patients when his master was out or disinclined.'[27] 'Although full-time practitioners labelled themselves as barber-surgeons or apothecaries, the common structure of apprenticeship was more significant than distinctions between them...'[28] Some gauge of their status is better made from an examination of the fees charged for taking on an apprentice (and also from the professions of the apprentices' fathers). Some masters charged as little as £20, while others could demand a sum ten times as high. John Townsend's substantial fee of £200 for training Richard Smith Snr. in 1762 implies that he was a surgeon of some considerable repute. Once they had served their seven-year term, apprentices were entitled to join the relevant city company, become freemen of the city and participate in elections. Until well into the eighteenth century, therefore, at least in the case of Bristol, it would in fact be a mistake to think of there being a 'medical profession' at all, if by this is implied a single cohesive identity and organisation.

As the century progressed, however, this state of affairs started to change. From the 1760s Infirmary-based surgeons started to take on pupils and pupilage slowly took over from apprenticeship as surgeons' prime means of training. Richard Smith Jnr. 'part of the first generation of hospital-trained surgeons',[29] was very dismissive of old-style apothecaries, whom he described as 'not men of education'. Indeed, he said, 'very many had been absolutely shop men and mortar boys.'[30] Fissell puts this attitude down to snobbery and the desire of surgeons (or at least Smith) by the end of the eighteenth century to associate themselves more closely with the 'gentlemanly' physicians, based in the Infirmary. One sign of this changed attitude was the tendency of surgeons already in practice to start taking MD degrees.[31] The hospital itself was becoming increasingly 'professionalized', i.e. increasingly run by the surgeons rather than the lay subscribers who had dominated its governance in the early years after its foundation in the 1730s. By the time Richard Snr. was elected by the subscribers in 1771, their place was becoming usurped more and more by the surgeons, and by his son's time was little more than honorary. The careers of Henry's father and brother illustrate these changes up to a point, though his father did receive hospital training in London after his apprenticeship and both Henry and Richard were apprenticed to their father when he died in 1791. Richard was then 'turned over' to Godfrey Lowe, a friend of the Smith family and successor to his father as Senior Surgeon to the Infirmary. There seems no definite evidence that his training under Lowe was a pupilage at the Infirmary rather than a traditional apprenticeship in his private practice but, given the date, the former seems more likely.

As already mentioned, Richard Senior had intended his sons to follow him into the medical profession, and both were indeed studying under him, but his sudden death changed these plans. 'Mr Henry Smith was removed altogether from the profession and was indentured to Mr Robert Payne, solicitor, in St John's Street.' No record of this indenture has yet come to light.[32] There were no attorneys in Henry's immediate family but it would not have been untypical for the son of a family of the Smiths' standing to enter the profession. During the eighteenth century the status of attorneys had been steadily rising, albeit from an initial position of disdain. Earlier in the century professional men in general were widely held in low regard. They were seen as parasites, not engaged in productive labour but making their living from the misfortunes of others. 'The doctors and lawyers especially, and among them the apothecaries and attorneys more particularly, were subject to the almost universal abuse of the satirists and commentators of the time, in plays, pamphlets, and novels'.[33] Blanket descriptions of the 'pretended Roguery and multitude of attorneys' were very common….and even their apologists believed that excessive numbers of attorneys tended to cause 'barratry' or the practice of stirring up vexatious suits... By contrast, the law's 'upper branch' of barristers and judges was normally believed to be above 'vile tricks' and mere 'pettifogging'.[34] However, as the century progressed rules relating to the training of attorneys became stricter. From 1729, legislation required that they serve a five-year clerkship[35] and the profession became increasingly regulated. By Henry's time, new entrants to the profession typically came from the professional and merchant classes as well as the minor gentry and yeomanry[36] and attorneys were an integral part of 'respectable society.'[37] By the early nineteenth century the term 'solicitor' was increasingly used.

Bristol was well stocked with attorneys; it may have been slipping down the rankings in terms of population and economic activity but with 71 in practice in 1800 it was behind only Liverpool among provincial cities.[38] The work of a provincial attorney at this time could be very varied, and might involve the management of estates and elections, the administration of local government and a range of financial business (though here the attorneys were beginning to lose business to the emerging local banks).[39] We have little detailed knowledge of Henry's work at this early stage in his career but by 1800, shortly after he qualified, he was assisting his aunt Martha Catcott in the management of the family estate at Fulham.[40]

Friends

Henry's friends, unsurprisingly, were drawn largely from the professional and merchant families of the city. Three of these feature prominently in the narrative of Henry's year on the run. **Peter Clissold**, who accompanied Henry in the early stages of his flight, was a fellow attorney. **Daniel Burges**, who went to enormous lengths to support Henry on his journey, was also an attorney and handled the arrangements for his defence. Henry seems to have known the family from childhood and curiously Dan's father, also Daniel, and City Solicitor of Bristol, had died in 1791, two months before Henry's father and at a similar age. At the time of the duel Daniel was in partnership with Robert Payne, Henry's old master. He was later to be a long-serving and well-respected town clerk of Bristol. His younger son, Edward, founded a firm of solicitors that has survived and still bears his name (Burges Salmon) and where Henry's defence brief for his trial is lodged. **James Lean** was a banker, the managing partner of Stuckey's Bank, then known as Stuckey, Lean, Hart and Co. which had opened in 1806 in Broad Quay.[41] The Lean family (James was married to Lucy, daughter of the bank's founder, Samuel Stuckey) then lived at 1, Belle Vue, where Henry had taken refuge on his return to Bristol in April. This was part of a new development of houses in Clifton that at the time lay uncompleted because of the disruption to the building industry caused by the war.[42] James was later Sheriff of Bristol (1833-4).

Militia and Freemasons

Along with many of his contemporaries Henry had fulfilled his patriotic duty by enlisting with the Royal Bristol Volunteers commanded by Colonel Evan Baillie. After disbandment in 1802 this had been reformed with great enthusiasm when the war was renewed in 1803.[43] This involved several weeks of duty each year. In 1808 Henry is listed as a lieutenant in the Grenadiers and his brother Richard as 1st Surgeon to the regiment.

Henry was also an active freemason. He had been proposed as a mason by James Lean in 1806 and a year later was appointed a Junior Warden of the Lodge of Hospitality.[44] Later he was to play a prominent role in the organisation.

Thomas Chatterton and the Smith and Catcott families

Chatterton knew both the Smith and the Catcott families. It was in the muniment room in St Mary Redcliffe Church that the poet 'discovered' the poems of Rowley which brought him such fame. Chatterton was wary of Alexander Catcott and avoided his company where possible, as from the start the latter had grave doubts as to the authenticity of his 'discoveries'. His brother George, however, had no such doubts: as Chatterton's one-time patron, and convinced of the authenticity of his 'discoveries', he was instrumental in bringing Chatterton's work to public attention, and was the initial publisher of the *Rowley* manuscripts. However, by 1770 the poet had fallen out significantly enough with both brothers for the following 'bequests' to appear in his will: 'Item: I give all my vigour and fire of youth to Mr George Catcott, being sensible he is most want of it … I leave the Reverend Mr [Alexander] Catcott some little of my free thinking, that he may put on spectacles of reason and see how vilely he is duped in believing the scriptures literally. I wish he and his brother George would know how far I am their real enemy; but I have an unlucky way of raillery, and when the strong fit of satire is upon me, I spare neither friend nor foe.'

He had also penned satirical poems about Henry's spinster aunt Martha, describing her as the 'Rose of Virginity'.

Chatterton was also intimately connected with the Smith family. Richard, Henry's father, and his brothers Peter and William were all one-time companions of the poet (indeed William Smith was his closest friend). On hearing of William's apparent suicide, Chatterton penned an 'Elegy on Mr William Smith' on 12th August 1769, with its declarations that he 'Loved him with a brother's ardent love.' At the bottom of the poem Chatterton has added the footnote 'Happily mistaken having since heard from good authority it is Peter [Smith]'.

Henry's brother later wrote: 'Peter Smith was another *bon compagnon*, and incurred by his irregularities with Chatterton, the displeasure of his father, so that he was most severely lectured; of which such was the effect, that he retired to his chamber and set to his associate an example that was but too soon followed … At first, Chatterton and [Richard] … were good friends, but the unhappy affair of his brother Peter estranged them, as Mr Smith attributed the wretched catastrophe to congenial opinions in morals and religion … William Bradford Smith was Chatterton's bosom friend.' Despite his suicide, Peter was buried at Temple Church 'in a vault in ye chansell'[34] on 14th August 1769.

There is a further reference to Henry's father in Chatterton's work *The Exhibition*, in which John Townsend, Richard's former master, is made to refer to his former apprentice as 'That thing of flatulence and noise, Whose surgery is but a heap of toys'.

'This, no doubt, was the poet's revenge on the young man, better educated than himself (whose name was blown about Bristol as a popular healer), for ceasing to know him.'[35]

APPENDIX 1

The nun's escape

Several stories arising from Henry Smith's and Ann's travels became part of family legend. Some of these may have become embellished in the telling. A striking example is this account of the escape of an Irish nun, Jane Power, which is recounted by Henry Rooth, Henry and Ann's grandson.

Tuesday 13th April 1909, Garrido's Hotel, Badajoz
Before closing the doings of an enjoyable day and leaving this part of Portugal [sic] I record an adventure in which my grandfather assisted which occurred at one of the towns we had visited to which he himself only makes a passing reference in his journal when at Badajos, tho' probably the incident took place at Lisbon, Belem or possibly Oporto. My mother often heard it from her father's lips and repeated the story to me, so I relate it that it may not be forgotten and as being almost worthy of Charles Lever the novelist.

   A century back the Portuguese nuns were strictly confined within the four walls of the convent and had but limited opportunity of conversing with the outside world. Such conversation being held through double gratings placed at such a distance it was only just possible for two persons without and within stretching out their arms to the utmost through the grating to touch one another's hands – these restrictions however had not prevented a British officer, a friend of my grandfather's, from falling passionately in love with a nun who reciprocated his feelings. She was Irish by birth – a Miss Power by name, though probably known by another in the convent and had taken the normal vows – the nun's name I have forgotten. Notwithstanding the awful risks (for the Inquisition exercised its cruel powers very fiercely in Portugal), she determined to break these vows and escape with her lover. It was however no easy task to devise a method by which she could do so and all conversation by reason of the distance which separated them was necessarily held with raised voice and therefore liable to be overheard. He took my grandfather into his confidence and on a certain night both arrived in a carriage with a ladder, ropes and a midshipman's uniform. The night was so black they could scarcely see the high wall which surrounded the convent and its garden which had to be scaled – not a sound could be heard – but at the last chimes of midnight a watch was flung over the wall from this garden – this proved to be Miss Power's and was probably the only article of jewellery allowed her. They hurriedly placed the ladder against the wall having now located her position and scaled it – trembling with terror. They hauled her up by the rope and dropped her silently down on the other side into the ditch. She availed herself of it and with a rapid change stood a few moments later metamorphosed into an English midshipman. They drove her away and with the cognisance of the captain she was taken in that uniform on one of King George's ships.

The news of her escape spread like wildfire. The officers of the Inquisition gaining a certain amount of information, perhaps from the coachman who drove, traced her to the fleet. Portugal was the ally of England fighting in a common cause. She insisted on the Church exercising its power of search which could not be resisted. Miss Power's position was terrible; if discovered she would have been seized without it being possible to raise a hand to prevent it and carried off to the direst penalties – probably ultimately being walled up alive.

At this terrifying moment a happy inspiration occurred to the ship's surgeon. Partially dressed in uniform he put the trembling girl in a dark midshipman's bunk placing several British naval officers only too willing to lend a helping hand round the bunk so that they should intervene between her and anyone entering the cabin. When the authorities of the Inquisition entered robed in sable and hideous terrifying black caps of penitence with their search warrant the surgeon held her wrist with one hand and his watch with the other whilst the naval officers stood hatless. Then placing his finger to his lips whispered 'schhh' looking heavenwards as tho' the spirit were just about to take its flight thither – and the poor creature doubtless with cheeks more ashen than the sheets she laid on lent truth to the situation. The authorities were hoodwinked and after making the sign of the cross bowed and took their departure. She was saved and subsequently became the mother of a large family.'[1]

This dramatic story may have some basis in fact but almost certainly did not involve Henry Smith. There is no suggestion or hint of such an event in the diary, although Henry did visit convents, spoke with nuns and witnessed contact between nuns and other visiting British officers. However there is an account of such an escape by Jane Power from an Irish convent in Belem although this probably happened some years before Henry's arrival in Portugal. See letter from Robert Southey to Charles Wynn, 8 January 1805, which relates such an incident with Jane Power dressed in men's clothing but with the escape organised by her brother-in-law; there is no mention of the Inquisition.[2]

1 Henry G. Rooth, *Journal in Spain and Portugal* (1909) pp. 187-89.
2 *Diaries of a lady of quality from 1797 to 1844,* ed. A. Haywood (London, 1864). Such a story could have circulated among the military in Portugal but also in Bristol where Robert Southey had been born in 1774.

APPENDIX 2

A note on duelling in Great Britain

Duelling probably reached its peak during the reign of George III (1760-1820)[1] and may have reached its high watermark during the early years of the new century: the enlarged armed forces provided fertile ground for disputes involving honour. But civilian life provided plenty of opportunity for quarrels. In 1809, quite apart from Priest and Smith's fatal meeting, there were three much better known encounters. Henry refers to the infamous duel between Castlereagh and Canning that took place in September and which ended with Canning being hit in the thigh. Castlereagh had insisted on a second round and since thigh wounds were often fatal Canning was fortunate the bullet went through the fleshy part of his leg.[2] In February the 9th Viscount Falkland was killed by a Mr Powell following a drunken and trivial dispute, and in May Colonel Cadogan fought with Lord Paget over Paget's affair with Cardogan's sister Lady Charlotte, wife of Henry Wellesley, one of Wellington's brothers. During his time in the Peninsula Henry Smith encountered several others who had fought or were to fight duels, among them Lieutenant John Blundell who was to meet his death in a contest in the Isle of Wight in 1813.

By 1800 sword fighting, at least in Britain, had become a rarity and pistols had become the norm. By this time the flintlock duelling pistol had become far more accurate than thirty years earlier although they could still be unreliable because the spark from the flint did not always fire the gun (merely causing a flash in the pan, as happened with Paget's pistol). Although the percussion cap had been patented two years before the Priest-Smith meeting it is highly unlikely they would have used such pistols.

The correct loading of pistols placed an additional responsibility on the seconds. The era when seconds were active participants in the fight had long passed, and by the time of the modern duel the role of the second had become 'an amalgam of umpire, cornerman and mediator'.[3] If at all possible the second's job was to ensure that the principals settled their differences without recourse to the duelling ground. Unfortunately Peter Clissold and Mr Guest had proved unpersuasive.

The rules for the engagement had to be agreed. How many shots were to be fired? Were the contestants to fire simultaneously? What signal should be given? How far apart should the duellists be? Ten to twenty 'paces' was the convention, but the length of the pace varied, some taking it as thirty inches, others as much as fifty. The approximate length of a cricket pitch would have been a fair guide, but often longer, and particularly vengeful hotheads were known to insist on much closer engagements with a high risk of death or injury.

It is impossible to get reliable figures on the risk of injuries and fatalities because many duels were unrecorded. 'A Traveller', writing in 1838 and cited by Richard Hopton, took a sample of 200 encounters and calculated the odds of being killed in a duel at 14 to 1 while the odds against injury were six to one.[4] Yet the 172 recorded duels during the reign of George III led to 69 deaths and 96 wounded. It seems highly likely that many duels were unrecorded and this would have been all the easier when there was no bloodshed.

There were only eighteen trials for duelling. Seven defendants were found guilty of manslaughter and three of murder of whom two were executed, one of them Major Campbell in 1808. Juries were reluctant to convict even when guided by judges to do so. In Henry's case Sir Vicary Gibbs made clear that since pre-meditation was involved in an arranged duel murder was the appropriate charge, not manslaughter. Yet honour had to be preserved; this made a challenge difficult to reject although Henry was fortunate he did not have to put these arguments to the test. The carelessness of the coroner allowed well-informed lawyers to expose the technical weaknesses of the charges against him.

Hopton points to the rapid decline of duelling in Britain after the 1820s as the growing influence of business led to increased respect for the rule of law: in a commercial society individuals resolved their differences in the law courts rather than on duelling grounds. By the 1830s Hopkins suggests duelling was looking increasingly archaic. Yet as late as 1829 Wellington, while Prime Minister, felt he had no choice but to issue a challenge to Lord Winchelsea, and Victor Kiernan records that fourteen duels were reported in *The Times* in the last three months of 1835.[5] The last duel known to be fought in England by Englishmen was in 1845 when Captain Seton was killed by Lt Hawkey following an incident in the King's Rooms in Southsea.[6]

APPENDIX 2

1. Richard Hopton, *Pistols at Dawn: A History of Duelling* (London, 2007). What follows relies heavily on this source.
2. John Campbell, *Pistols at Dawn: Two Hundred Years of Political Rivalry from Pitt and Fox to Blair and Brown*, (London, 2010) pp. 57-89.
3. Hopton, p. 53.
4. Ibid, p. 95.
5. V.G. Kiernan, *The Duel in European History: Honour and the Reign of Aristocracy* (Oxford, 1988) p. 204.
6. Andrew Steinmetz, *The Romance of Duelling in all Times and Countries* (London, 1868), vol II pp. 367-9. The argument was about Seton's attentions to Hawkey's wife. The last known duel was in 1852 in Old Windsor between two Frenchmen.

APPENDIX 3

Dramatis Personae

United Kingdom
Baillie, Evan (c.1742-1835), of a prominent Bristol family of merchants, bankers and West Indian landowners, was Colonel Commandant of the Royal Bristol Volunteers.
Bird, Robert (c.1761-1846). Attorney, Andover.
Bleeck, John (1773-1860). Wool merchant, Warminster. Relative of Henry Smith.
Burges, Daniel (1776-1864). Attorney, later (from 1822) City Solicitor and Town Clerk for Bristol. Father, also Daniel, was founder of Bristol Law Society. Practised in partnership with William Brice. His son, Edward, qualified as a solicitor in 1837 and founded, in 1841 as sole practitioner, the firm that later became Burges Salmon. Partner with Robert Payne, Glastonbury. Agent Heelis. Father (Daniel) died 1791. Very favourable description in Latimer, p. 214.
Catalani, Angelica (1779/1780-1849). Italian opera singer. Latimer: 'equally famous for her voice and her rapacity', p. 96 on 1822 visit to Bristol.
Clarke, William Lenton. Joint Deputy Registrar of Bristol.
Clayfield, William. Chemist (and balloonist). A balloon flight from Bristol in September 1810 ended in a forced landing in the sea near Lynmouth (Latimer, pp. 40-1).
Clissold, Peter. Attorney, Brislington.
Cornish, William. Tea Dealer, Clare Street, Bristol.
Dampier, Henry (Sir) (1758-1816). Barrister and Judge. KC 1813 and knighted 1813. An outstanding lawyer, prominent on the western circuit, he had worked with Sir Vicary Gibbs and knew him well. See judgement at Lymington (in July 1814 he was the judge in a case where a duellist, Captain W.H. Souper, was convicted of murder, in line with his strong lead to the jury; he was sentenced to hang, but it appears that Souper made such an impressive and affecting plea for mercy that Dampier recommended clemency).
Duggan, Walter. Brazier, a client of Henry who witnessed the duel.
Garrow, William (Sir), (1760-1840). Barrister and KC, Lincoln's Inn. Well-known barrister but undistinguished judge and law officer. Later

Solicitor-General (1812-13) and Attorney-General (1813-17), knighted 1817. J. M. Beattie, 'Garrow, Sir William (1760–1840)', *Oxford Dictionary of National Biography*, Oxford University Press, 2004. [www.oxforddnb.com/view/article/10410, accessed 30 June 2011]

Gibbs, Sir Vicary (1751-1820), whose 'incivility, condescension, and sarcasm earned him the nickname Vinegar Gibbs', was Attorney-General at the time. R.A. Melikan, *Oxford Dictionary of National Biography*, Oxford University Press, 2004; online edn, Oct 2009 [www.oxforddnb.com/view/article/10608, accessed 29 Oct 2012] (see Blundell entry)

Gurney, John (Sir) (1768-1845). Barrister and Judge. KC 1816 and knighted 1832. Sergeant's Inn, Fleet Street.

Heelis, Thomas. Attorney, Staples Inn. Henry Smith's London agent.

Hetling, William. Surgeon, Orchard Street, Bristol.

Hunt, Henry ('Orator') (1773-1835). At this time (1808-9) Hunt, who was a considerable landowner, spent most of the winter months in Bath; but he had built a 'sporting' cottage, Sans Souci, on his estate in Wiltshire and 'I devoted the summer and autumn to the sports of the field, particularly shooting, of which I was passionately fond, and which this country afforded in the greatest perfection'. *Memoirs of Henry Hunt, Esq. vol. 2.*

Kerr, Mrs John. Lodging House Keeper, 81 Cathcart Street, Greenock. Sister of Rev. McDougall.

Lean, James. Born 1783 or 1784, died 1849. He was managing partner of Stuckey's Bank (Stuckeys, Lean, Hart & Co.). Known as Stuckeys, Lean, Hart & Maningford by 1811 and later as Stuckey, Lean & Co. He was son-in-law of Samuel Stuckey, and married to Lucy. Among their children was Vincent Stuckey Lean, author of *Collectanea*, who at his death in 1899 bequeathed £50,000 for construction of the Bristol Central Library. Lived at 1 Belle Vue at time of Henry's visit in 1809. P T Saunders, *Stuckey's Bank* (Taunton: Barnicott & Pierce, 1928).

Lippincott, Sir Henry (1773-1829) was Colonel Commandant of the North Gloucester Militia. Tried for rape on 10 April 1810 – not guilty. According to Latimer, 'a somewhat debauched representative of the old Bristol family of Cann' (Latimer, p. 39).

Ludlow, Ebeneezer, (c.1777-1851). Barrister. Special pleader. Oriel College, Oxford. Barrister at law, Gray's Inn, 1805. Sergeant at law 1827, KC and QC. Town clerk of Bristol 1819, and commissioner of bankruptcy 1842.

Described colourfully and unfavourably by Latimer, e.g. pp. 213-4.
Lyon, James. Merchant, McIvers Land, Mansion House Lane, Greenock.
McDougall, John. 81, Cathcart Street, Greenock, Lieutenant, 91 Highlanders (probably Ensign). Nephew and lodger of Mrs. Kerr.
McDougall, Rev. Archibald? Lochgoilhead. Brother of Mrs. Kerr.
Newman, Richard N. Doctor, St Michael's Hill, Bristol.
Payne, Robert. Attorney, Bristol and Glastonbury. Partner of Dan Burges in 1809 Law list. Listed 1798 and 1809 Law lists. Henry Smith's 'master'.
Robe, Archibald. Merchant, 40, Park Street, Bristol.
Skelton, 'Captain'. 81, Cathcart Street, Greenock. Possibly either Lt. Charles Cornwallis Skelton or Lt. Jeremiah Skelton.
Smith, Joseph. Barrister, Montague Parade, Bristol.
Smith, Richard (1772-1843), Henry's elder brother. Surgeon, later chief surgeon of the Bristol Royal Infirmary
Swayne, John. Surgeon, 15 Cumberland Street, Bristol.
Thompson, John. Greenock.
Whitchurch, Samuel. Park Row, Bristol.
Yeatman, Morgan. Surgeon, 11, Cumberland Street, Bristol.

Military (Peninsula)
Beresford, William Carr. (1768-1854). Marshall in the Portuguese Army and in charge of reforming it.
Blantyre, Lord Robert. (1777-1830). Lt. Col. 42nd Foot (Black Watch). Later Major-Gen. Gold Medal, CB.
Blundell, John. Lt. 7th Foot. Later, in 1813, less than a month after marrying, he was killed in a duel in Newport, Isle of Wight. The surviving principal (Ensign Edward McGuire) and the seconds were all convicted of murder and sentenced to death by Justice Sir Vicary Gibbs but a royal pardon was granted.
Browne, John. Capt. 1st Line. Wounded Badajoz and Waterloo. Died 1849.
Campbell, John. Capt. 42nd Foot (Black Watch). Later (1815) Lt. Col. Wounded Orthes. Gold Medal, CB. Died 1841.
Campbell, William Howe. (1783-1852). Capt. 23rd Foot. DAQMG Nov. 1809. Later Major-Gen.
Cole, Galbraith, Sir 1772-1842. Colonel, later General. Gold Medal KCB Had been in India with Wellington.
Darroch, Duncan. (1776-1847). Colonel, 36th Foot. AAG. Later General.

Düring, Georg von. Lt. KGL. Adj.-Gen Office. Later Lt. Gen.
Ferguson, Capt. 41st Foot. Possibly Dugald, listed as Captain with 95th in Nov. '09. Killed Salamanca, 1812.
Fry, George. Lt. 83rd Foot. Later Capt. Killed Badajoz 6 April 1812.
Glascott, William. Lt. 16th Light Dragoons. Resigned 1812.
Henderson, John. Lt. 42nd Foot (Black Watch). Later (1811) Captain. Died of wounds received at Toulouse, 1814.
Kelly, Dawson. (?1782-1837). Capt. 27th Foot. DAQMG. Later Col.
Leighton, Burgh. Col. 4th Dragoons. Gold Medal.
L'Estrange, Isaac Francis. Capt. 3rd Foot. Cashiered: GCM Nov. 1812.
Madden, George Allan, Sir (1771-1828). Brigadier-General, in 1809 commander of a Portuguese Cavalry brigade. He had fought a duel with a brother officer in 1804. CB, knighted 1816.
McArthur, Peter. Lt. 3rd Foot. Later (1810) Captain 14th Line.
Mercer, Douglas (assumed surname of Henderson). Capt. 3rd Footguards. Later (1813) Lt. Col. CB. Died 1854.
Sherbrooke, Sir John Coope. (1764-1830). Lt. Gen. 68th Foot and 2nd in command to Wellington.
Somerset, Lord Edward. (1776-1842). Lt. Col. Commander of 4th Dragoons, later General, had a particularly distinguished record in the Peninsular campaigns and at Waterloo. Gold Cross.
Stewart, Sir Charles. (1778-1854). Maj-Gen. Adjutant-General. Half-brother of Lord Castlereagh; later, as Sir Charles Vane, he was 3rd marquess of Londonderry. Of unquestionable bravery, he was not entirely trusted by Wellington as a commander.
Stewart, Charles. Possibly Col 23rd Dragoons.
Symons, Henry John, Rev. (1781-1857). Chaplain 1st Footguards. Fellow of St. John's College, Oxford. Awarded DCL 1813 before returning to Peninsula and becoming Chaplain to Forces. He became Rector of St. Martin, Hereford and in 1857 died of a heart attack when running for a train.
Tidy, Francis Skelly. (1775-1835). Major, 14th Foot. Later (1813) Lt Col.
Waters, John (Sir). (1773/4-1842) Lt. Col., he was one of Wellington's intelligence officers who had played a vital role at the Battle of Oporto by discovering some hidden boats that enabled the army to cross the Douro. Later Lt. Gen. Gold Cross, CB, knighted 1832.

Notes

Introduction
1 For example, *Bristol Evening Post*, 16 August 1934, 'Pistols for Two: Fatal Local Duel'.
2 Henry Smith, 'Journal in Spain and Portugal, 1809-10', MS C214, Spencer Library, University of Kansas, Lawrence, Kansas.
3 It is mentioned in a letter John wrote to his brother James Augustus Rooth.
4 HG Rooth, 'Journal in Spain and Portugal', Ms, 1909.
5 'Bristol Gaol Delivery 1810: The King against Henry Smith'.
6 Bristol Record Office, 35893/36, Papers of Richard Smith.

chapter 1
1 Henry Hunt (1773-1835), later widely known as Orator Hunt.
2 *Bristol Gazette*, 23 Feb. and 2 March 1809, *Farley's Bristol Journal*, 25 Feb. 1809, and *Bristol Mirror*, 25 Feb. 1809, and Playbill, 20 Feb. 1809. Kathleen Barker Collection, University of Bristol. But Catalani knew how to charge, and later in the year her high salary was a central cause of the 'old price riots' of Covent Garden, leading one recent commentator to describe her as 'the loathed opera singer'. Tracy C Davis, *The Economics of the British Stage 1800-1914* (Cambridge, 2000), p. 26. The Bristol prices were far higher than those that caused such trouble at Covent Garden.
3 Evidence of William Lewton Clarke, Solicitor, and Samuel Whitchurch, Merchant, 'Brief for Defendant'.
4 Although not mentioned in the diary, Henry and Peter were also accompanied by another second, Archibald Robe. 'Brief for Defendant'.
5 Messrs. John Swayne and Morgan Yeatman.
  The Bolt-in-Tun (now demolished) was one of the main coaching inns of London, situated at 64, Fleet Street.
6 These have survived and are now in the Hammersmith and Fulham Archives.
7 Nearly £3000 in today's purchasing power and more than ten times that amount in relation to contemporary earnings. Lawrence H. Officer and Samuel H. Williamson, 'Purchasing Power of British Pounds from 1245 to Present,' *Measuring Worth*, 2011. www.measuringworth.com/ppoweruk.

chapter 2
1 i.e. 'muggins'.
2 Built from 1735 and opened as The Tontine Hotel in 1781, it was situated at Glasgow Cross and next to the Exchange, which originally took place on the street outside. Pulled down c.1904 and replaced by the present edifice.
3 Built in 1801 and later serving as the Post Office, it was pulled down c.1900 and replaced by the James Watt Inn, which still stands today (2012).
4 Probably the 'Mrs John Kerr, boarding-house keeper' living at 81, Cathcart Street (opposite the Tontine Inn) in 1815 (*Directory of Greenock*, 1815-1816).
5 Probably that 'Mr James Lyon, merchant' living at McIvers Land, Mansion House Lane in the 1815 *Directory of Greenock*.
6 A glee society.
7 i.e. 'I am doomed' (*Othello* Act 3, Scene 3).

NOTES

chapter 3

1 Dr Symons' account appeared in *Notes and Queries* (1852, no. 151), p. 274 and makes clear that the burial took place in daylight and not at dead of night as recorded in the poem by Charles Wolfe that immortalised the event. See also James Moore, *A Narrative of the Campaign by the British Army in Spain* (London, 1809), pp. 366-7.
2 A graphic first-hand description of the terrible conditions during the retreat can be found in *The Recollections of Rifleman Harris*, edited and introduced by Christopher Hibbert (London, 1970).
3 Rory Muir, *Britain and the Defeat of Napoleon 1807-1815* (New Haven and London, 1996), pp. 60 and 80-81.
4 Muir, *Britain and the Defeat of Napoleon*, pp. 84-6.
5 Captain John Browne, 4th Foot or Royals.
6 He also had about 2,400 Portuguese troops.
7 A barber rowed across from the north bank and alerted Colonel John Waters, one of Wellesley's observation officers, to the three (by some accounts four) wine barges. These were then brought across to the south bank by Oportans and the Buffs embarked on a hazardous daylight crossing, each barge taking about thirty soldiers. The failure of French forces to spot the river crossing may in part have been because they had expected the British to advance from the west.
8 This account does not mention that the French were advancing up the steep hill and were also being shelled from the British artillery on the south bank.
9 But Soult lost far more on the retreat. Julian Paget, *Wellington's Peninsular War: Battles and Battlefields* (London, 1996 edition, p. 89), records 300 killed and wounded as well as 1500 taken prisoner and 70 guns. There were 123 British casualties.
10 General Murray might have cut off the retreat but failed to do so. There was some pursuit, notably by the 14th Dragoons, but lack of transport was a major obstacle to a more general pursuit.

chapter 4

1 A view shared, among others, by Lord Byron who had been in Lisbon in July 1809.
'What beauties doth Lisboa first unfold!
Her image floating on that noble tide ...
But whoso entereth within this town,
That sheening far, celestial seems to be,
Disconsolate will wander up and down,
'Mid many things unsightly to strange ee;
For hut and palace show like filthily:
The dingy denizens are rear'd in dirt;
No personage of high or mean degree
Doth care for cleanness of surtout or shirt;
Though shent with Egypt's plague, unkempt,
unwash'd, unhurt.'
Byron, *Childe Harold's Pilgrimage*
2 Madden had himself fought a duel in 1804 but, having taken his opponent's shot, had fired in the air.
3 Gordon L Teffeteller, 'Beresford, William Carr, Viscount Beresford (1768–1854)', *Oxford Dictionary of National Biography*, Oxford University Press, 2004; online edn, Jan 2011 [http://www.oxforddnb.com/view/article/2199, accessed 29 Dec 2011]. Rory Muir, 'Wellington and the Peninsular War: The Ingredients of Victory', in Muir et al, *Inside Wellington's Peninsular Army 1808-1814*, pp. 3, 7-8.

4 Translated as: 'In the reign of Dom João V, the best of kings, the benefactor of Portugal, safe and healthy water supplies were brought to the city of Lisbon along aqueducts strong enough to last forever, and measuring nine thousand yards in length, the work being carried out at reasonable public expense and with the sincere gratitude of everyone. In the year of our lord 1748'. On Pombal's initiative this had replaced an earlier inscription placing more weight on the people's contribution and less on that of the king! José Saramago, *Journey to Portugal* (Harvill, London, 2000) pp. 347-8.

chapter 5

1 Wellesley had in fact been raised to the English peerage as Baron Douro of Wellesley and Viscount Wellington of Talavera on 26th August (gazetted 4th September).
2 This opinion was later to be bloodily refuted in the sieges of 1811 and the costly re-taking of the town in 1812 (the British and Portuguese army had departed from Spain in 1810).
3 A Forlorn Hope refers to the first wave of troops storming a breach during a siege: the risk of death or serious injury was high but the leading officer, if he survived, would gain not only glory but almost certainly promotion too.
4 Wellington made several journeys to Lisbon that winter to inspect the Lines of Torres Vedras, a vast defensive barrier being constructed under the supervision of Lt Col Richard Fletcher to protect the city.
5 Not to be confused with the great university city of the same name in Castile, this town has not been identified and may be the result of confusion on Smith's part.
6 Not to be confused with Talavera de la Reina where the battle had been fought in July.

chapter 6

1 Smith is not using the correct title which should have been Baron Douro of Wellesley and Viscount Wellington of Talavera.
2 This is an exposed and dangerous position but it gives volunteers an opportunity to distinguish themselves in combat and therefore, if they survive, the chance of a commission.

chapter 7

1 Thomas Cox, *Magna Britannia et Hibernia: Somersetshire* (1720-31) p. 745, cited by W E. Minchinton, *The Port of Bristol in the Eighteenth Century* (Bristol, 1962), p. 2.
2 Minchinton, *Port,* pp. 1-8.
3 www.localhistories.org/bristol.htm; K Morgan, 'The Economic Development of Bristol, 1700-1850' in M. Dresser and P. Ollerenshaw (eds.), *The Making of Modern Bristol* (Bristol, 1996), p. 49.
4 J Barry, 'Bristol Pride: Civic Identity in Bristol c.1640-1775', in M Dresser and P Ollerenshaw (eds.), *The Making of Modern Bristol* (Bristol, 1996), p. 25.
5 Morgan, 'Economic Development', p. 49.
6 R.A Buchanan and Neil Cossons, *The Industrial Archaeology of the Bristol Region.* (Newton Abbot, 1969) pp. 16–19.
7 John Latimer, *The Annals of Bristol in the Nineteenth Century* (Bristol, 1887), p. 1. Bernard Alford also emphasises the role of entrepreneurial weakness in Bristol's relative decline and the 'intensely obscurantist' attitude of the Corporation to economic and social affairs. BWE Alford, 'The economic development of Bristol in the nineteenth century: an enigma?' in Patrick McGrath and John Cannon (eds) *Essays in Bristol and Gloucestershire History* (Bristol, 1976) pp. 261-3.
8 MD Lobel and EM Carus-Wilson, *The Atlas of Historic Towns: Bristol* (London, 1975),

NOTES

pp. 1-2.
9 Minchinton, *Port*, p. 23.
10 Lobel and Carus-Wilson, *Historic Towns*, p. 23.
11 JE Tunbridge, 'Spatial change in high-class residence: the case of Bristol', *Area*, Vol. 9: 3 (1977), pp. 171-4.
12 Prerogative Court of Canterbury wills, 1609.
13 This quotation and the following accounts of Richard's life (where not otherwise noted) are taken from his son Richard Smith Junior's 'Biographical Memoirs' (MS), Bristol Record Office Ref. 35893/36.
14 A considerable sum for an apprenticeship, suggesting that Townsend was a surgeon of some repute (see Fissell, p. 49).
15 It is now known as St. Bartholomew's Hospital and still stands at the bottom of Christmas Steps.
16 Nigel Aston, 'Catcott, Alexander Stopford (1692-1749)', *Oxford Dictionary of National Biography*, Oxford University Press, 2004 [www.oxforddnb.com/view/article/4879, accessed 21 May 2011]
17 She had a sister, Martha, and a much younger brother, Thomas, described as a 'mere accountant'.
18 JS Chamberlain, 'Catcott, Alexander (1725–1779)', *Oxford Dictionary of National Biography*, Oxford University Press, 2004 [www.oxforddnb.com/view/article/4878, accessed 21 May 2011].
19 'Nor less is fam'd the bridge, whose arches stride
O'er the dull surface of thy turbid tide.
Since Catcott first, (who fights to gain a name,
And madly climbs up half-built spires to fame)
Cross'd o'er the pile with proud triumphant air,
And risk'd his life to make the stupid stare'
Robert Lovell, *Bristol: A Satire* (1794) from A. Beeson *Bristol in 1807: Impressions of the city at the time of Abolition* (Bristol, 2009) p. 60.
20 Although Chatterton died by his own hand it is not clear whether this was suicide or the result of an accidental overdose: Nick Groom, 'Chatterton, Thomas (1752-1770)', *Oxford Dictionary of National Biography*, Oxford University Press, 2004 [www.oxforddnb.com/view/article/5189, accessed 24 May 2011]. E.H.W. Meyerstein, *A Life of Thomas Chatterton*, (London, 1930), ch. 18. The Smith family were also connected with Chatterton. More detail follows in an appended note.
21 GB Munro, *A History of the Bristol Royal Infirmary* (London, 1917), p. 463.
22 Ibid, p. 97, quoting Richard Smith's *Memoirs*.
23 This is the equivalent of £160,000 when measured against 2009 prices and over £2 million when expressed against average earnings. EH.Net. Lawrence H. Officer and Samuel H Williamson, 'Purchasing Power of British Pounds from 1245 to Present,' *Measuring Worth*, 2011. www.measuringworth.com/ppoweruk
24 Copy of an article by Stanley Hutton entitled 'Forgotten Bristol Worthy', probably from a local Bristol newspaper. It is undated but was published shortly after the presentation of an oil portrait of Smith (by TD Taylor) to the Municipal Art Gallery (probably c.1905). Cutting from Paul Rooth of Brighton. Richard is remembered today, if at all, chiefly for his role in the gruesome story of John Horwood, hanged for the murder of his lover Elisa Balsam, whose life Richard had tried to save. After his execution, despite the best efforts of Horwood's family, Richard retrieved the body and performed a public dissection of it. He then wrote an account of the trial and had it bound in the murderer's skin, dyed a tasteful shade of green.

25 Mary E Fissell *Patients, Power and the Poor in Eighteenth-Century Bristol* (Cambridge, 2002), p. 50.
26 Bernice Hamilton, 'The Medical Professions in the Eighteenth Century', *Economic History Review* 2nd Series, vol. IV (1951), p. 141.
27 Fissell, pp. 48-49.
28 Ibid.
29 Ibid, p. 55.
30 Quoted in Ibid, p. 56.
31 Ibid, p. 62.
32 I was advised by officials at the Bristol Record Office on a visit on 8th September 2009 that Henry's indenture would probably have been a private contract between individuals rather than part of a formal process involving the city authorities, explaining its absence from the records. He does not appear in the Burgess Books 1786-1812 (FCI/BB/17/2 (indexes) or CE/BB/1 (v) 1-8 (records)
33 R Robson, *The Attorney in Eighteenth-century England*, (Cambridge, 1959), p. 134.
34 D Lemmings, *Professors of the Law: Barristers and English legal culture in the eighteenth century* (Oxford, 2000).
35 CW Brooks, *Lawyers, litigation, and English society since 1450* (London, 1998).
36 Ibid.
37 Robson, p. 146.
38 Ibid, pp. 166-7.
39 M. Birks, *Gentlemen of the Law*, (London, 1960) quoted by MJ Pritchard, Review, *Cambridge Law Journal*, 18 (1960), pp .242 ff.
40 Catcott (Fulham) estate: scrapbook, NRA 16811, Reference DD/109, Accession 109, Hammersmith and Fulham Archives.
41 PT Saunders, *Stuckey's Bank* (Taunton, 1928).
42 Latimer, *Annals*, p. 10.
43 Edwin T Morgan, *A Brief History of the Bristol Volunteers from the earliest recorded formation to the establishment of the Territorial Army in 1908.* (Bristol, 1908?).
44 Lodge of Hospitality Transactions, 1806 and 1807. Library, Freemasons Hall, Park Street, Bristol.
45 Registers of Temple Church, quoted in Meyerstein.
46 Ibid.

Bibliography

NEWSPAPERS
Bristol Evening Post, 16 August 1934
Bristol Gazette, 23 February, 2 March 1809, 19 and 26 April 1810
Bristol Mirror, 25 February 1809 and 21 April 1810
Farley's Bristol Journal, 25 February 1809 and 21 April 1810

MISCELLANEOUS PAPERS
Bristol Gaol Delivery 1810: The King against Henry Smith. Burges Salmon Archives
Catcott (Fulham) estate: scrapbook, NRA 16811, Reference DD/109, Accession 109, Hammersmith and Fulham Archives
Lodge of Hospitality Transactions, 1806 and 1807. Library, Freemasons Hall, Park Street, Bristol
Playbill, 20 February 1809. Kathleen Barker Collection, University of Bristol

DIRECTORIES
Bristol, 1808, 1809, 1811, 1812 and 1814
Greenock, 1815-16

BOOK, ARTICLES AND MANUSCRIPT MATERIAL
ALFORD, B.W.E. 'The economic development of Bristol in the nineteenth century: an enigma?' in Patrick McGrath and John Cannon (eds) *Essays in Bristol and Gloucestershire History* (Bristol, 1976) pp. 252-283.
ASTON, Nigel Catcott, Alexander Stopford (1692-1749), *Oxford Dictionary of National Biography* (Oxford University Press, 2004) [www.oxforddnb.com/view/article/4879, accessed 21 May 2011]
BARRY, J. 'Bristol Pride: Civic Identity in Bristol c.1640-1775' in M. Dresser and P. Ollerenshaw (eds.), *The Making of Modern Bristol* (Bristol, 1996)
BEESON, Anthony *Bristol in 1807: Impressions of the city at the time of Abolition* (Bristol, 2009)
BELCHEM, John '*Orator' Hunt: Henry Hunt and English Working-Class Radicalism* (Oxford, 1985)
BYRON, Lord, 'Childe Harold's Pilgrimage', *The Works of Lord Byron* (Wordsworth edition) (Ware, 1994)
BIRKS, M. *Gentlemen of the Law* (London, 1960) cited by M.J. Pritchard, Review, *Cambridge Law Journal*, 18 (1960), pp. 242 ff.
BROOKS, C.W. *Lawyers, Litigation, and English society since 1450* (London, 1998)
BUCHANAN, R. A. and COSSONS, Neil, *The Industrial Archaeology of the Bristol Region* (Newton Abbot, 1969)
CHALLIS, Lionel S. *Peninsula Roll Call* 1949. *The Napoleon Series* www.napoleonseries.org
CHAMBERLAIN, J.S. Catcott, Alexander (1725–1779), *Oxford Dictionary of National Biography* (Oxford University Press, 2004) www.oxforddnb.com/view/article/4878, accessed 21 May 2011]
DAVIS, Tracy C. *The Economics of the British Stage 1800-1914* (Cambridge, 2000)
DRESSER, Madge and OLLERENSHAW, Phillip (eds.), *The Making of Modern Bristol* (Bristol, 1996)
FISSELL, Mary E. *Patients, Power and the Poor in Eighteenth-Century Bristol* (Cambridge, 1991)
GROOM, Nick 'Chatterton, Thomas (1752–1770)', *Oxford Dictionary of National Biography*, (Oxford University Press, 2004) [www.oxforddnb.com/view/article/5189, accessed 24 May 2011]
HAMILTON, Bernice, 'The Medical Professions in the Eighteenth Century', *The Economic History Review* (2nd Series, Vol. IV, 1951) pp. 141-169.
HAYWOOD, A. *Diaries of a lady of quality from 1797 to 1844* (London, 1864)

HIBBERT, Christopher (ed), *The Recollections of Rifleman Harris* (London, 1970)
HOPKINS, Richard, *Pistols at Dawn: A History of Duelling* (London, 2007)
HUNT, Henry *Memoirs of Henry Hunt, Esq., vol. 2* (written by himself in his Majesty's Jail at Ilchester 1820-22)
KIERNAN, V. G. *The Duel in European History: Honour and the Reign of Aristocracy* (Oxford, 1988)
LATIMER, John *The Annals of Bristol in the Nineteenth Century* (Bristol, 1887)
LEMMINGS, D. *Professors of the Law: Barristers and English legal culture in the eighteenth century* (Oxford, 2000)
LOBEL, M.D. and E.M. CARUS-WILSON *The Atlas of Historic Towns: Bristol* (London, 1975)
LONGFORD, Elizabeth *Wellington, The Years of the Sword* (London, 1969)
MEYERSTEIN, E.H.W. *A Life of Thomas Chatterton* (London, 1930)
MINCHINTON, W.E. *The Port of Bristol in the Eighteenth Century* (Bristol, 1962)
MOORE, James, *A Narrative of the Campaign by the British Army in Spain* (London, 1809)
MORGAN, Edwin T. *A Brief History of the Bristol Volunteers from the earliest recorded formation to the establishment of the Territorial Army in 1908* (Bristol, c.1908)
MORGAN, K. 'The Economic Development of Bristol, 1700-1850' in M. Dresser and P. Ollerenshaw (eds.), *The Making of Modern Bristol* (Bristol, 1996)
MORGAN, Kenneth 'Bristol West India Merchants in the Eighteenth Century', *Transactions of the Royal Historical Society*, (3, 1993) pp. 185-208
MUIR, Rory *Britain and the Defeat of Napoleon 1807-1815* (New Haven and London, 1996)
MUIR, Rory 'Wellington and the Peninsular War: The Ingredients of Victory', in Muir et al, *Inside Wellington's Army.*
MUIR, Rory; BURNHAM, Robert; MUIR, Howie, and MCGUIGAN, Ron *Inside Wellington's Peninsular Army 1808-1814* (Barnsley, 2006)
MUNRO, G.B. *A History of the Bristol Royal Infirmary* (London, 1917)
OFFICER, Lawrence H. and Samuel H. WILLIAMSON, 'Purchasing Power of British Pounds from 1245 to Present', Measuring Worth, 2011. www.measuringworth.com/ppoweruk
PAGET, Julian *Wellington's Peninsular War: Battles and Battlefields* (London, 1996 edition)
PARTRIDGE, Richard, and OLIVER, Michael *Napoleonic Army Handbook: The British Army and Her Allies* (London, 1999)
ROBSON, R. *The Attorney in Eighteenth-century England* (Cambridge, 1959)
ROOTH, Henry G. *Journal in Spain and Portugal* (1909) MS.
SARAMAGO, José *Journey to Portugal* (London, 2000)
SAUNDERS, P.T. *Stuckey's Bank* (Taunton, 1928)
SMITH, Henry *Journal in Spain and Portugal, 1809-10*, MS C214, Spencer Library, University of Kansas, Lawrence, Kansas
SMITH, Richard Papers, Bristol Record Office, 35893/36
STEINMETZ, Andrew *The Romance of Duelling in all Times and Countries* (London, 1868) vol II.
SYMONS, Henry J. 'The Burial of Sir John Moore', *Notes and Queries*, no. 151 (1852), p. 274.
TEFFETELLER, Gordon L. Beresford,' William Carr, Viscount Beresford (1768-1854)', *Oxford Dictionary of National Biography* (Oxford University Press, 2004); online edn, Jan 2011 [www.oxforddnb.com/view/article/2199, accessed 29 Dec 2011]
TUNBRIDGE, J.E. 'Spatial change in high-class residence: the case of Bristol' *Area*, Vol. 9:3 (1977), pp. 171-4.
URBAN, Mark *Rifles: Six Years with Wellington's Legendary Sharpshooters* (London, 2003)
WARD, S.G.P. *Wellington* (London, 1963)
WARD, S.G.P. *Wellington's Headquarters: A Study of the Administrative Problems in the Peninsula 1809-1814* (Oxford, 1957)